*Yoga natural foods
can change your life!*

Like millions of Americans, you're
concerned about the foods you eat.
Chances are, most of them
contain chemical additives that destroy
vital nutrients . . . dull your taste . . .
deplete you of physical and emotional vitality.

YOGA NATURAL FOODS COOKBOOK
offers a delicious dietary alternative to today's
adulterated foods. The first complete book
of its kind, it provides
you with a rich assortment of natural
foods indispensable for better health and
better eating. Foods that are not
denatured, processed, pickled
or otherwise rendered totally useless.

Learn from a famed Yoga teacher how to
prepare over 250 fresh-from-Nature recipes—
desserts, salads, snacks, main dishes—simply,
quickly, delectably. Ways to bring out the
delicate flavor of "life-force" foods. Yoga food
secrets for staying young,
keeping your weight down and your energy up.

More than a cookbook, there's an exciting
experience in natural nutrition that
will reawaken your taste—
and change you dramatically in body and mind.

YOGA NATURAL FOODS COOKBOOK

BY
RICHARD HITTLEMAN

BANTAM BOOKS · TORONTO · LONDON · NEW YORK

A NATIONAL GENERAL COMPANY

YOGA NATURAL FOODS COOKBOOK
by Richard Hittleman

A Bantam Book/published by arrangement
with Workman Publishing Company, Inc.

Bantam edition published September 1970
2ND printing
3RD printing
4TH printing
5TH printing

Published simultaneously in the United States
and Canada

Bantam Books are published by Bantam Books, Inc., a National
General company. Its trade-mark, consisting of the words "Bantam
Books" and the portrayal of a bantam, is registered in the United
States Patent Office and in other countries. Marca Registrada.
Bantam Books, Inc., 666 Fifth Avenue, New York, N.Y. 10019.

PRINTED IN THE UNITED STATES OF AMERICA

TABLE OF CONTENTS

INTRODUCTION

You've seen the headlines recently:

MONO-SODIUM GLUTAMATE (MSG) BANNED!
99 PESTICIDES BANNED!
CYCLAMATES OFF GROCERS' SHELVES!

We fervently hope that this is only the beginning and that in the coming years our federal agencies will continue to seriously investigate the dozens of additives, pesticides, and contaminants that are used to preserve, color, fumigate, age, bleach, stabilize, emulsify, smoke, pickle or thicken *about 97% of the food items in the supermarket!* Read the labels and you will find sulphur dioxide, magnesium chloride, sodium alginate, monoisopropyl, benzoic acid, dimenthyl polysiloxane, stilbestrol, coal-tar dyes, ammonium chloride, mono and diglycerides, polyoxyethylene, aluminum sulphate, sodium nitrate and calcium hydroxide are common additives, one or more of which has been infused into just about every food item you pick up in your market. We are told that these chemical agents are "safe in small quantities"—just as we were formerly told that poisonous pesticides, monosodium glutamate and cyclamates were "safe."

But chemicals comprise only part of the food tragedy. Vital nutrients are also being methodically destroyed through the various commercial processes used in growing, refining, cooking, canning, bottling and packaging. The more efficient these processes become for the producer, the more nutritional destruction that seems to occur. However, the consumer is, at long last, beginning to awaken to the gravity of the situation: that his food supply may well be of low nutritional quality and that it is certainly polluted with chemicals. What most consumers have yet to learn is that *there is an alternative to a diet of adulterated foods;* it is the diet of the Yogi which provides the perfect, natural alternative.

The science of Yoga, offering a program of natural development for body, mind, and spirit, considers nutrition of paramount importance and has evolved, through the centuries, a philosophy of eating which today deserves the most serious attention of every American.

The Yogic concepts of what constitutes *true nourishment* differ in a number of important respects from those with which most people in the western world are familiar. In addition, the objectives of eating transcend simply nourishing the body and sustaining life. Here is what is involved: the aim of the student of Yoga, through his practice of the exercises, breathing and meditation, is to experience states of joy, awareness and of peace. It is imperative that his diet does not in any way detract from this high level of well being but, rather, that it *complements* his goals. He must, therefore, select those foods which will regenerate and impart vitality to the body with a minimum of stress, and which will leave the mind clear and elevated. The nutritional principles which are applied in realizing these objectives are so effective that they will prove of inestimable value not only to the Yoga student who aspires to derive the greatest benefits from his practice, but to all those readers who recognize that an alternative to the "typical American diet," replete with chemical additives and denatured foods is essential. They realize, too, that the way they look, feel and function are directly related to what they eat.

In Yoga philosophy we learn that all life is developed and sustained through *prana,* a Sanskrit term which can be translated as "life-force" or "pure energy." The more life-force that your organism is able to assimilate and utilize, the more physical health and vitality, the more mental alertness, the more emotional stability, and the more spiritual awareness you come to possess. The entire practice of Hatha Yoga is concerned with: (1) Gaining access to the storehouse of prana already existent within the organism but which lies dormant, asleep, waiting to be aroused; (2) Introducing an abundance of prana into the organism from external sources. The techniques for accomplishing both these objectives form the subject matter of this series of books. A major source of prana, *food,* is of such great importance that it warrants this separate volume.

Which are the life-force foods? *Natural foods —primarily those which grow.* We designate vegetables, herbs, fruits, nuts, grains, legumes and certain dairy products, "natural." "Natural eating" is consuming these foods either in their natural state or in a state that renders them fit for easy digestion with minimum destruction of their life-force.

To the extent that natural foods are *denatured,* that is, refined, canned, preserved, smoked, aged, colored, fumigated, stabilized, thickened, "enriched," and processed, as well as cooked through such methods as frying and boiling, they are devitalized, rendered lifeless from our viewpoint. You can fill your stomach with these substances and, if you have grown sufficiently desensitized through years of use and abuse, feel "satisfied." But, according to Yogic theory, the true elements of nourishment, of life-force, are minimized. For example, the fact that you do not immediately drop dead after finishing a typical seven-course restaurant dinner does not necessarily mean that you are receiving genuine nourishment from that meal. It is rather a testimonial to the remarkable strength of the organism, to how much abuse it can withstand day after day, year after year, and still survive. But "survival" is not comparable to existing in the elevated state of which we have spoken—the state of vitality, mental keenness, emotional health and spiritual richness.

The crux of the matter is this: what you eat can either impart great life-force, vitality, help to regenerate the body, regulate your weight, have a profoundly positive effect on your mind and emotions, or can sap life-force, add excess weight, cause premature aging, be a contributing factor in many illnesses, and greatly lower the vibrations of the entire organism.

When I lecture on Yoga Nutrition I name groups of denatured foods that include several thousand items from the supermarket. Often, before I finish, some distressed listener will interject, "But you're eliminating everything. There's nothing left to eat!" On the contrary. When denatured foods are excluded from the diet an entire world of nutrition that heretofore has been hidden will emerge. The average person seldom consumes more than 150 different foods each week, about 90% of which are denatured. This book offers our carefully-tested methods for preparing a much greater number of *only natural foods* in many delicious ways, making them easy to digest with the minimum destruction of their life-force.

You'll find sections on how to find and select life-force foods—from vegetables and fruits through beans and grains. You'll read about what foods are good for you and which are not, which to avoid—and why. Then you can go on to the recipes, and because of their wide scope and variety, you will see that it is possible, practical and simple for you and your family to follow the all-natural Yoga diet on a permanent basis, without reverting to denatured, adulterated foods. And to your great surprise, you'll find that with strong seasonings and heavy sweeteners removed, your taste buds will be free—perhaps for the first time—to really savor the delicate nuances of flavor natural (and hopefully organically-grown) food offers. For the first week, you can if you choose to, follow our menus.

It is not our intention to deprive you of the

11

"fun" of eating, but rather to have you experience both the delight of natural food nutrition and the dramatic changes that it will make in your body, your mind, and your spirit.

—RICHARD HITTLEMAN
Carmel, California

I
ALL ABOUT YOGA
NATURAL FOODS

The following pages classify the
various types of foods. Each category
contains important notes which will
clarify the Yogic principles of
selection and preparation. Study this
before proceeding to the recipes.

VEGETABLES

A large percentage of the Yogi's daily diet consists of vegetables, both cooked and raw. All edible vegetables contain vital nutritional elements and are a prime source of life-force. Unfortunately, the methods of preparation employed by most cooks (chefs as well as housewives) render the vegetable not only lifeless but tasteless. To compensate for this flatness in flavor, sauces, dressings and spices are added, turning what has become just so much pulp into something which, in many cases, is also indigestible.

The theory underlying this type of preparation seems to be: "Since vegetables are good for you, the form in which they enter the digestive system is of little consequence. Because they are being eaten, we will derive their inherent nutritional benefits. The way to make sure they are eaten is to appeal to the taste buds." From our Yogic viewpoint this theory is most destructive. *The form in which foods enter the digestive system is of the greatest possible concern.* Hollandaise sauce on asparagus, sour cream and butter on potatoes, roquefort dressing on salads, destroy whatever life-force might still remain in the vegetables after they have been grown in inorganic soil, sprayed with pesticides, chemically colored, and overcooked.

From the time the infant is first introduced to baby foods, the emphasis is on appeal to the taste buds (ironically, not to the infant's taste buds but to the mother's!). Very quickly the taste buds of the child are satiated with the various condiments so that natural, subtle flavors cannot be appreciated. Fruits, vegetables, nuts, dairy products, and meats that are not artificially sweetened, salted, spiced, pickled, etc. taste "flat" and are avoided. When eating is predicated on pleasing dulled taste buds, the intake of life-force will be reduced to a minimum and this eventually results in the manifestation of more negative physical conditions than can be enumerated here. In the Yoga nutrition program the taste buds are given a respite from strong and artificial condiments so that they become purified; then, if vegetables are selected and prepared correctly, to retain their life-force, they will be found extremely flavorful, requiring only small amounts of natural seasonings, if desired, to make them delicious and satisfying.

In selecting vegetables our first choice is, of course, those which are fresh. The best fresh vegetables are those which are *organically grown* and unsprayed, either in your own garden or that of a reputable grower. The term "organic" refers to soil that has been prepared with a natural compost rather than with chemical fertilizers. "Organic" also implies the absence of pesticides. Unfortunately, organic produce is not plentiful because of the economics involved; it is available in some health food stores, at some farms and, occasionally, in markets that are in the proximity of large produce areas. The flavor and quality of organic produce is superior to the inorganic, although its color and size are not always as appealing. Take the time to search out whatever organic produce may exist in your area. A very small plot of land will enable you to plan your own organic garden. The philosophical as well as practical advantages of your own vegetable garden deserve your most serious consideration and literature on "Organic Gardening" is easy to find.

When fresh produce is unavailable, frozen vegetables can be substituted. For our purposes, vegetables in cans and jars are without value and are not to be used.

A sub-classification of vegetables available in the United States and Canada will facilitate our discussion.

**Vegetables which are the
fruit of the plant:**

Tomatoes, cucumbers, squashes, peppers, eggplant, pumpkins. These vegetables are low in calories and contain varying amounts of potassium, sodium, calcium, magnesium, iron, phosphorus and sulphur. Tomatoes, peppers, and cucumbers, good sources of vitamin C, can be steamed, baked or eaten raw. These are also used for "cleansing" purposes by the the Yogi.

16

Starch Vegetables:

Potatoes (all varieties: Irish, Idaho, sweet), artichokes. Squashes may also be included here. Do not be put off by the word "starch." This is starch that is needed and well utilized by the body. The common variety of potato is made up of water, a small amount of protein, starch and cellulose. The sweet potato (yam) also contains cane sugar. Baking is the best method of cooking these vegetables. It is imperative that, whenever possible, the skins of the potato be consumed. The elements in the skins balance the starch of the interior. Wash and scrub very well before baking. Overweight people may eat *only* the skin to good advantage.

Green Vegetables:

Lettuce (all varieties), celery, chard, spinach, endive, mustard greens, cabbages (all varieties, including broccoli, cauliflower), watercress, dandelion greens and all other green, leafy vegetables. These are very rich in life-force. They should be eaten in liberal amounts each day, raw in salads with dressings as indicated in the recipes and/or very lightly *steamed*. Never boil or overcook these valuable green vegetables. Even when steamed they must remain tender and crisp, the consistency being similar to that of the vegetables served in a Chinese restaurant. Correct steaming time for the various vegetables is easily learned.

Root and Bulb Vegetables:

Carrots, turnips, onions (all varieties), beets, parsnips, radishes, garlic, leeks, chives, rutabagas, asparagus, horseradish. All of the statements pertaining to the Green Vegetables also apply to this category. The water in which a

17

vegetable has been steamed can contain important nutritional elements. It may be served as a broth seasoned with vegetable salt, or used as a stock for a thicker soup. The broth can be refrigerated for no more than two days.

Sprouts:

Bean, alfalfa, mung, soy. Very, very high in life-force. Nourishing, easily digested, a source of quick energy. At least one of these sprouts is now available in packaged form in most markets. Sprouts have a multitude of uses in vegetable dishes, salads, sandwiches and as snacks. They can even be used as a substitute for fresh vegetables during the winter months.

Bean, grain or seed sprouts can be easily generated at home. There are several methods. Here is a simple one:

Obtain a one quart jar with a wide mouth. Place the substance to be sprouted in the jar, cover with water and soak overnight. (See amounts below.) Secure a double layer of cheese cloth over the top of the jar with a rubber band. Run water through the cloth and rinse the seeds thoroughly. Drain all water from jar. Next, shake jar so that seeds adhere to the sides. Place jar in a warm, dry, dark place. Each morning and evening for the next two days rinse as described above. On the third day you will have sprouts (there will be some variance in time according to what you are sprouting). Place the jar in sunshine for about an hour to absorb chlorophyll. If sunshine is unavailable sprouts may be used as is. Refrigerate whatever is not used. The amounts suggested below will supply an average family with sprouts for several days. Mung beans—6 tablespoons; Soy beans—10 tablespoons; Alfalfa seeds—2 tablespoons; Lentils—8 tablespoons. You can experiment with any grain or seed.

Miscellaneous:

Fungi: mushrooms. Seaweed: kelp, dulse, carageen. Mushrooms make an excellent entrée as our recipes will show. Serve them raw in salads. Seaweed, a most nutritious substance, is available in Oriental and gourmet markets.

Incidentally, if you have access to an Oriental market you will find many fascinating, delicious vegetables. Bamboo shoots, water chestnuts, and snow peas are a few that you should try steamed.

Remember that all vegetables which are not organically grown require very thorough washing. Soak for as long as possible before using and then rinse thoroughly. A tablespoon of cider vinegar added to the soaking water will aid in the removal of the pesticides.

Yoga nutrition calls for at least one meal each day to include *both* a raw salad and one or more cooked vegetables. Many ways to prepare and combine both raw and cooked vegetables for maximum life-force are offered in our recipes.

Vegetable Juices:

These are another prime source of life-force and are quickly assimilated. Pure vegetable juices are obtained with the use of a juice extractor and contain no additives. They are bottled commercially and can be purchased at health food stores. However, to insure freshness, quality, and superior flavor, you should have your own extractor. For example, a number of our recipes call for "tomato juice." It would be ideal to use fresh tomato juice which you extracted or the relatively fresh, unadulterated bottled product available in health food stores. The same holds true wherever vegetables or fruit juices are indicated in the recipes.

An extractor manufactured by a reputable firm is an excellent investment in health and of particular value to Yoga students who undertake a periodic juice fast. Extractors are generally available at larger appliance stores. (The pulp that is produced in the juicing process makes for excellent natural compost in an organic garden.)

SEASONINGS

In Yoga nutrition strong seasonings are avoided. These are without value and are used strictly for catering to the taste buds. They do not bring out the flavor in foods but simply alter natural flavors and will often destroy the life-force of foods. We want to avoid not only the digestive disturbances caused by harsh spices and those seasonings, dressings, sauces, and various concoctions that contain chemical additives (catsup, relish, etc.) but the agitation and restlessness that are disturbing to the mind. The mind cannot be considered as an entity apart from the body; they are interrelated to the degree that whatever effects one has a corresponding effect on the other. Even if we were to disregard the eventual damage that can be done to the stomach, liver, and kidneys we must be aware that when the digestive system is irritated it is difficult for us to maintain the type of control over the mind and emotions that is essential for the Yoga student. Indeed, the controlled and quiet mind is of such importance in the practice of meditation that Yogic literature dating from many centuries past cautions specifically against the use of harsh, irritating spices. These spices would include salt, pepper, mustard, chili, vinegar and curry powder. Since salt (sodium chloride) is the basic element of the American diet, its complete absence from our recipes requires a few words of explanation.

Salt dries, hardens, constricts, ossifies and tightens. It is excellent for helping to pickle and preserve. Consequently it is used by processors and packagers to retard decay and add to the shelf life of nearly every packaged food item in the market.

But what does this sodium chloride, which never grew, which never had life, do to the living tissues of our organisms? Are they not also dried, ossified, in short, "pickled"? The deadly effects of sodium chloride are well known to those persons who must now adhere to a salt-free diet. *The body does require organic salts* and these are supplied from an adequate consumption of natural foods as provided by our recipes. The natural salts that may be used for seasonings are listed below.

In addition to being irritants, strong seasoning agents produce excessive thirst, requiring the intake of much larger quantities of fluid than would otherwise be necessary. We do not consider this desirable.

Almost all ready-made salad dressings that are available in the markets are not to be used. You will be hard put to find one such product that does not contain salt, harsh condiments and chemical additives. In light of our preceding discussion you can see the absurdity of using such lifeless products on your freshly-made raw salad. For seasonings, we will utilize the mild herbs, fresh garlic, onions, parsley, lemon juice, soy bean sauce, sea salt, celery and vegetable salts (derived from a combination of vegetables and available in health food stores). We also make extensive use of the unsaturated oils including olive, safflower, sesame, soy, etc. Unless specified, a recipe calling for "oil" refers to any one of your favorite unsaturated oils. Also, unless specified as "celery" or "vegetable" a recipe calling for "salt" refers to sea salt.

LEGUMES

The foods in this category are an excellent source of protein and include all varieties of fresh and dried peas, beans (blackeye, lima, kidney, soy), St. John's Bread, peanuts, pistachios. (Also see "Nuts and Seeds.") One good serving of legumes can provide sufficient protein for a meal. Prior to cooking dried peas, beans, and lentils it is advisable to soak them overnight.

The soy bean and its by-products are very high in protein. Crushed soy beans produce soy "milk" which has been a staple for centuries in the Far East. Soy milk powder is available mostly in the health food stores. The method for making soy bean cakes (tofu) is included in our recipes. We make sparing use of soy bean "sauce" as a seasoning.

The pod of St. John's Bread is eaten and the

bean usually discarded; the pod is good exercise for the teeth. When St. John's Bread is ground it becomes an excellent flavoring powder, "carob," which can be used as a malt base for nourishing drinks and as a healthful sweetening agent for general use.

Because of their density, it is advisable to consume legumes in moderation.

FRUITS

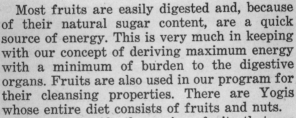

Most fruits are easily digested and, because of their natural sugar content, are a quick source of energy. This is very much in keeping with our concept of deriving maximum energy with a minimum of burden to the digestive organs. Fruits are also used in our program for their cleansing properties. There are Yogis whose entire diet consists of fruits and nuts.

We can classify the various fruits that are available to most of us at different times of the year as follows:

Acid Fruits (also known as "citrus" fruits):
Oranges, grapefruits, lemons, limes, tangerines, pineapples; we also include the strawberry, raspberry, loganberry, and cranberry. Although we refer to these as "acid" fruits, once consumed they have an alkaline effect. Many of the acid fruits require a subtropical

climate for growth. The orange and grapefruit are important because of their high content of vitamin C. This essential vitamin does not store in the body and must be replaced daily. The orange is exceptionally high in fruit sugar which is ready for immediate assimilation. The grapefruit is excellent for cleansing purposes, as is the juice of the lemon and lime. The latter two are strong and should be used in small amounts. We recommend them frequently in salad dressings. Many students have eaten only one or two grapefruits at breakfast for a week at a time and found the resultant feeling of lightness and alertness to be most gratifying.

Acid fruits and their juices (orange, grapefruit, pineapple, tangerine) should not be combined with the usual breakfast foods such as ham, bacon, eggs, toast, coffee. From our viewpoint the value of the citrus fruits and juices is nullified in this mixture. Citrus fruits combine well with one another and can be mixed to advantage with certain proteins such as nut butters. The juices should be freshly squeezed, either by yourself, or where you can see it done, since we know that a large amount of the value is lost if the juice stands for even a half hour. The value of the frozen concentrated citrus juices is questionable for our purposes.

A dish of any of the berries mentioned above makes an excellent breakfast.

Here is a hygienic suggestion that has proven valuable for many of our students: Upon arising in the morning, mix the juice of a half lemon, freshly squeezed, with about four ounces of spring water. Drink and wait for several minutes; then perform five rounds of the Abdominal Lift Exercise. This procedure will aid in proper elimination. This simple routine is done in the following way:

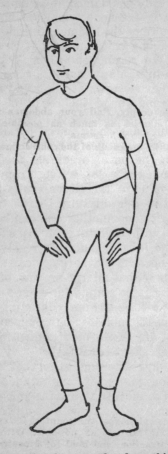

Fig. 1. Standing, rest hands on thighs.

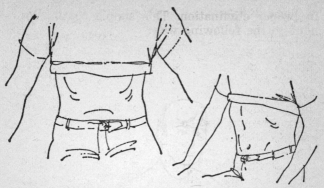

Fig. 2. Exhale deeply. Pull your abdomen in by contracting the muscles as much as possible. Hold for 5 counts.
Fig. 3. A closeup of the contraction.

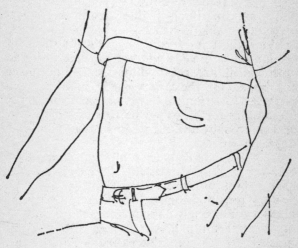

Fig. 4. Upon completion of the count of 5, try to "snap" the abdomen as far out as possible. Without pause, repeat the contraction, and hold for 5 counts. Perform 5 times. Stand up slowly.

Subacid Fruits:

Apples, apricots, peaches, guavas, persimmons, pomegranates, nectarines, pears, cherries, plums, grapes, melons, papaya, mangoes, blueberries, bananas, avocados, coconuts, olives, watermelons. When in season, it is often desirable to make a complete meal of these fruits. One may combine and eat as many of these as he wishes. Such a meal will always leave you feeling light and alert. Many Yoga students will eat only fresh subacid fruits for several days during one of the summer months for purposes of cleansing. This is referred to as a "fruit fast."

There is a popular misconception regarding such fruits as coconuts, bananas, and avocados. It is thought that these fruits will add excess weight to the body. However, the oils and fats which are contained in these fruits are necessary and highly beneficial and should not add excess weight *if correctly combined with compatible foods*. People who eat an avocado salad with a steak and potato dinner should not place the blame on the avocado for adding extra pounds. Nutritionists have calculated that man could exist for extended periods of time solely on the coconut and its milk, so high are their nutritive value.

All skins must be very thoroughly washed. If heavy spraying of pesticides is suspected it is best to peel and discard the skins.

Very few of the subacid fruit juices that are bottled for market distribution are of value to us. They contain sugar and chemicals. Some brands of apple, grape, and prune juice are exceptions. *Read the labels.* Health food stores are the best source of commercially bottled, unadulterated juices. Your own blender and juice extractor can provide you with "nectar of the Gods" from the subacid fruits.

Dried Fruits:

Dates, figs, raisins, prunes. These are wonderful, handy sources of immediate sugar energy. They can be used most satisfactorily in place of refined sugar candies. Children should be encouraged to eat these rather than the usual commercial candies, cakes and other between meal snacks. They make an excellent lunchbox item. Other fruits can also be "dried" such as the apricot and peach. A mixture of dried fruits, soaked overnight in water, makes a satisfying breakfast during the winter months. Raisins and dates can be used in cereals and salads. *Do not consume the dried fruits that have been preserved with sulphur dioxide.* All health food stores and some markets have the dried fruits without preservatives.

Cooking is generally unnecessary for fruits although some, such as the apple and pear, may be baked. Fruits may be combined, to advantage, with such proteins as cheeses and nuts or nut butters. It is also feasible to mix certain fruits with raw vegetables for a highly nourishing salad; apples and raisins, for example, combine well with lettuce, cucumbers, carrots, and celery.

Since fruits in jars and cans have very little value for our purposes, rely chiefly on whatever *fresh* and dried fruits are available. Frozen fruits are our second choice. Always try to obtain those frozen fruits that have the least sugar, additives, preservatives, etc. *Read the labels.* Ideally, we want *none* of these additives in any of the foods we consume.

DAIRY PRODUCTS

Milk

In our program we do not believe that the large quantities of milk suggested by the various dairy organizations for daily consumption are necessary. We also contend that because of the various processings to which milk is subjected many of its nutrients are better derived from other sources given in this book. However, milk is included in a number of our recipes and here are the types we prefer: Certified raw milk —milk which is pure and which has been properly inspected but not pasteurized (boiled) and homogenized (separated); fresh or powdered nonfat milk (from which the fat has been removed); evaporated milk, sparingly. Certified raw milk (and cream, if desired) can be obtained at health food stores and from certain dairy companies (ask your milk delivery man). Nonfat and evaporated milk are readily available in almost every market and are lower in cost. Unless definitely specified, "milk" in our recipes means that you may use either raw or nonfat.

Yogurt

Yogurt is rich in lactic acid and aids in digestion and elimination. In its various forms yogurt has been used for centuries by peoples of the Balkan countries and, in the last decade, has become very popular in the United States. We believe it to be a superior dairy product. Many health food stores have the "culture" and directions for making your own yogurt. It's easy to do. Homemade yogurt is an exceptionally delicious and nourishing food. You can obtain yogurt in most markets and grocery stores. Avoid those yogurts that are flavored with syrups and other additives. The entire value of yogurt lies in its fermentation and if this process is properly executed the product must have a slightly tart taste. But the reasoning of most dairy companies seems to be: "People have heard that yogurt is good for them but many may not like the tart taste, so we'll add syrups and flavorings and make it palatable for everybody." And what happens to the value of the yogurt? Apparently it doesn't matter as long as the taste buds are pleased. I recently noticed the crowning achievement of this reasoning in a local market: "chocolate flavored" yogurt! Revolting? It could be only the beginning. Hot fudge, banana split yogurt may be just over the horizon—and a small amount of aspirin could be added just in case you have a headache.

If you feel that "plain" yogurt is too Spartan try vanilla yogurt with various fruits and vegetables, as a base for salad dressings and as a flavorful topping for cereals. We use yogurt in many ways in our recipes. We always prefer the "plain" type.

Sour cream, which some people equate with yogurt, is actually quite high in fat content. We have used it sparingly.

Butter

Butter is exceptionally high in fat content. We will make use of the polyunsaturated margarines; however, we prefer those that have no artificial flavoring, coloring, and sodium benzoate. Again, for the pure product we must refer you to the health food stores. Pure butter made from certified raw milk is also available in the health food stores. This is a delicious product but very rich, so it must be used sparingly. But if pure butter is ever desired, this is the best product.

Cream

Sweet cream, and half and half are also, of course, very high in fat content. Occasionally, ice cream is a good dessert, especially if you learn to make your own, using raw sugar or honey, certified raw cream, and natural flavoring. (See Dessert recipes.) Some health food stores carry these ice creams.

Cheese

Many cheeses are subjected to processing which makes them undesirable for us. They are high in fat, aged, seasoned with salt and other condiments, and contain preservatives. We suggest low fat cottage, farmer, hoop, ricotta (Italian), feta (Greek), natural Swiss and Wisconsin cheddar. All of these cheeses combine well with fruits and vegetables and are good sources of protein. None of the commercial cheese "spreads" are desirable. Read the labels and you will understand why.

We make use of parmesan cheese primarily for seasoning. For certain spreads, dressings, and whips we use cream cheese, sparingly. The recipes include Homemade Cream Cheese.

PROTEINS AND FLESH FOODS

Proteins are the building materials of which all living tissue is composed. It consists of about 50% carbon, some hydrogen, oxygen, nitrogen, traces of sulphur and occasionally phosphorus and iron. From these elements nature builds *amino acids*. In Yoga nutrition it is not enough to know that protein is necessary in the diet. *There are different types and qualities of protein.* It is this essential fact that must be examined if we seek to learn which proteins are of the greatest value to us.

In recent years the consumption of large amounts of protein has been heavily advocated, especially as a method for weight loss. We believe that excess amounts of concentrated protein, especially in the form of animal products, results in only a temporary solution to a weight regulation problem. We think of the high protein diets as setting the body on fire. The fire may burn away some weight and also impart the illusion of energy. But the flame must be kept high or the energy disappears and the weight returns. In the long run these diets do not increase but rather deplete vitality, and possibly health. The Yogi seeks to maintain a small, steady, controlled flame through adequate quantities of high quality protein. Therefore, while meats, poultry, eggs, and milk are high in *quantities* of protein, the Yoga student derives his *quality* protein from cheese, nuts, nut butters, yogurt, legumes, avocados, coconuts, olives, and whole grains. This preference is based on both physiological and spiritual principles; these should be briefly examined.

Animals are slaughtered to provide flesh foods. In addition to his aversion to killing, the Yogi believes that there can be no life-force derived from a dead creature. In Yogic theory, meat inhibits the activation of the life-force and lowers the vibrations of the mind and spirit. To test this statement I have suggested the following experiment to many of my beginning students:

A period of thirty days is set aside during which a person who has been including flesh foods in his diet will eat no meat, poultry or fish whatsoever. The natural proteins listed above are substituted. In the course of the thirty days a subtle, gradual change occurs: he becomes light in body, keen in sense perception and alert in mind. At the termination of the thirty-day period he indulges in one of his typical former meat dinners with all of the usual trimmings. The intense letdown and heaviness that occur physically and mentally following this meal is dramatic. It reveals to the student, in the most direct possible manner, the effect that meat has upon the organism. This *feeling* is more convincing than all of the debate that he can get into regarding the efficacy of meat eating.

Anyone who has been a heavy meat eater and undertakes our Yoga nutrition suggestions often craves (much more in his mind than his body) a meat meal. I advise him to go along with our recipes for the thirty-day period mentioned above and then, if he continues to crave flesh food, have his meat dinner. Let him then determine whether his energy level and awareness are raised or lowered in the twenty-four-hour period following the meat meal.

You should become familiar with some of the facts of modern beef production. The typical steer is synthetically conceived, synthetically fed (with waste products from various sources included in its feed mixture), grazes for only a brief period, if at all, on grassy ranges, and ingests large doses of antibiotics. Surely one must seriously question how much nourishment is to be derived from this creature after it is slaughtered, frozen, shipped, further dissected, "tenderized" and then cooked. Obviously, such "food" cannot conform to Yogic nutritional principles. The uric acid, fibres and general acidity of meats always make their digestion a chore. And it appears that the packagers of so-called "luncheon" meats have carried the art of additives and preservatives to its ultimate refinement. *Read the labels.*

Poultry fares little better. Antibiotics are included in its quick fattening diet and injections of stilbestrol are administered to produce soft, tender flesh.

It is still possible to obtain some fresh, whole fish that has escaped the chemical fate of meat and poultry. However, this relative purity may not obtain for long if water pollution continues at its current rate.

We offer no recipes for flesh foods. This would be contrary to our entire theory. The serious student of Yoga realizes the necessity of eliminating them from his diet. Those readers who are not Yoga students but are anxious to see what Yoga Nutrition can do for them will certainly be able to go for at least the thirty days suggested above without flesh foods and will solve whatever problems may relate to this abstinence. Those readers who feel it *is* necessary to consume meat can find all the recipes they need from other sources. Of course it must be evident that including flesh foods in the diet will definitely decrease the effectiveness (physical and spiritual) of Yoga Nutrition.

EGGS

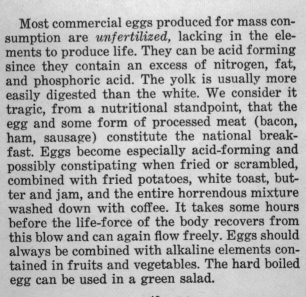

Most commercial eggs produced for mass consumption are *unfertilized*, lacking in the elements to produce life. They can be acid forming since they contain an excess of nitrogen, fat, and phosphoric acid. The yolk is usually more easily digested than the white. We consider it tragic, from a nutritional standpoint, that the egg and some form of processed meat (bacon, ham, sausage) constitute the national breakfast. Eggs become especially acid-forming and possibly constipating when fried or scrambled, combined with fried potatoes, white toast, butter and jam, and the entire horrendous mixture washed down with coffee. It takes some hours before the life-force of the body recovers from this blow and can again flow freely. Eggs should always be combined with alkaline elements contained in fruits and vegetables. The hard boiled egg can be used in a green salad.

Fertilized eggs contain the elements to support life and are always to be preferred to those that are unfertilized. Fertilized eggs are available at health food stores, some markets and some farms. It is worth your time to seek them out. The flavor is much superior.

Because of their "binding" qualities we use eggs in our recipes primarily for batters.

We should note here that many Yogis in India will not consume either eggs or milk, considering both to be animal products. This avoidance is often dependent upon the other types of food available in a particular geographical region. If you wish to do so, you may undertake a complete diet, as available through the recipes of this book, without including either eggs or milk.

NUTS AND SEEDS

Our primary source of plant protein is nuts. Pound for pound, many nuts contain as much or more protein as milk or meat. Moreover, for our purposes, nuts are preferred to meat as a complete food. In addition to protein, they contain vitamins, mineral salts, sugar, starches and oil. The fat of nuts is not to be confused with animal fats; the former is in an emulsified state and a valuable element which can be quickly and easily digested *if the nut is not mixed with incompatible foods*. (Most animal products and processed foods are incompatible.)

Almonds, pecans, cashews, brazils, walnuts, and coconuts are available to most of us throughout the year. However, they must be consumed in an unroasted, unsalted state. The processing of nuts, which includes roasting, adding salt, butter and preservatives, seriously reduces their life-force and can render them indigestible and fattening. Therefore, they must be consumed as close as possible to their natural state, simply shelled and, if necessary, skinned, but always unroasted and unsalted. Nuts must be chewed thoroughly.

You cannot think of nuts as between-meals or after-meals snacks. They are too much of a food. Nuts can comprise the major protein of any meal and they combine well with fruits or raw vegetables. In our recipes we have indicated the use of nuts and seeds in salads.

Nut butters are of equal value; they are delicious and very high in protein. Almond and cashew butters are currently available in health food stores and make good sandwich spreads. You may temporarily use the lightly roasted (but unsalted) almond and cashew butters until you become accustomed to the raw nut flavors.

The peanut is classified as a legume, not a nut; it is different in composition. However, we should note here that unsalted, lightly roasted peanut butter is also available and is to be preferred to the salted products.

Remember, we want to make certain that we do not consume *too much* protein, so when we include a fair number of nuts in a meal, we must go lightly on any additional protein foods at that meal.

Seeds are also excellent sources of protein. Sunflower, chia, pumpkin and sesame are just a few of the many varieties that are pleasant and nourishing. They should be consumed unroasted and unsalted, and can be sprinkled on many fruit and vegetable dishes. Being light, nourishing and satisfying, a handful of seeds can serve as a between-meal snack for quick energy.

BEVERAGES

Water is the number one source of life-force that we ingest. It must be pure—fresh or bottled spring water or tap water without chemicals. We extend due appreciation to those municipal organizations who have so thoughtfully arranged for chemicals to be added to our drinking water; however, we prefer ours *pure*. The frightening possibilities of fluoridation have been detailed by many authorities and if you don't know what they are, you should become informed. However, if you and your family are drinking fluoridated water you should certainly decide whether you wish to continue doing so by reading some of the easily-obtained literature. I personally prefer to prevent tooth decay through the elimination of refined, processed, adulterated foods and to obtain necessary minerals from natural foods rather than chemicalized water.

Water for drinking and cooking must be

pure. If necessary, have large bottles of spring water delivered or buy smaller bottles in the store. Remember: whenever we call for "water" in our recipes *we mean pure water*. This is very important.

All fresh fruit and vegetable juices are high in life-force. Squeeze, extract and blend juices with your own appliances if possible. Health food stores carry bottled fruit and vegetable juices which are probably a few days old and therefore contain less life-force, but they are to be preferred to all canned, frozen and concentrated juices. "Punches" and drinks to which sugar and chemicals have been added are to be avoided. Some brands of grape, apple and prune juices available in the markets are without additives. *Read the labels*.

Vegetable broths derived from the steaming of your vegetables are very nourishing and can be drunk as a tea.

Fruit juices derived from the baking or stewing of fruits such as apples, pears, apricots, and raisins are delicious.

Herb teas are favorite drinks of the Yogi. A great variety of subtle flavors are available in health food stores. These teas have many healthful properties.

All colas, whether regular or low-calorie, are to be avoided. The syrups and chemical sweetening agents used in these products are, from our viewpoint, life-force killers. The same applies to all commercial ice cream beverages (malts, shakes, sodas).

The Yogi eliminates all beverages that contain artificial stimulants, since they produce effects that are diametrically opposed to the principles of Yoga. Coffee, tea, colas and alcohol

45

are examples of such stimulants. The caffein in coffee and the bromine in tea are stimulants that have an adverse effect on the nervous system. They are addicting. Because you receive an artificial "lift" from a cup of coffee (due to the effect of the caffein), you are soon drinking four to eight cups or more each day. This must eventually have a telling effect on the nervous system, usually resulting in irritability, depression and insomnia. These states are not conducive to the practice of Yoga in which a calm, steady, controlled nervous system is of primary importance. If you want to "kick" the stimulant habit, substitute low caffein, cereal beverages, herb teas and the other natural beverages listed above.

Alcohol artificially relaxes and/or exhilarates. When its effects wear off, the body is left heavy and inert and the mind usually dulled and depressed. (Light white and red wines, the least harmful of the alcoholic beverages, may be exceptions.) The dependence upon alcohol to attain a sense of false relaxation and exhilaration is, from the Yogic viewpoint, unwise and unnecessary. The natural elation, optimism and exuberance of the organism with an abundance of life-force cannot be duplicated by any intoxicant or drug. As you continue to follow your Yoga program of exercises, meditation and nutrition you will almost certainly notice that the desire for all artificial stimulants, including alcohol disappears or is greatly reduced. The organism, attaining a state of natural exuberance and joy, automatically rejects such stimulants because it has no need for them.

No beverage should ever be consumed at extreme temperatures—ice cold or boiling hot. We advise against the use of ice cubes in drinks.

There should be as little drinking as possible *during* a meal because the liquid interferes with digestion. If necessary, drink before your meal and then allow your food to digest before drinking again. If you eliminate strong seasonings, and if you include salads and fruits in your meals, you will have all the fluid you need.

GRAINS
(Bread—Cereal—Rice)

Wheat, rye, barley, oats, millet, corn, and rice
are grains. Most commercial flours and cereals
are derived from grains that have been grown
in soil with pesticides. These grains are quick-
ground, refined, bleached, "enriched," disin-
fected, salted and preserved. If the two most
vital parts of the kernel—the embryo (wheat
germ) and the bran layers—are removed, what
life-force can remain? These are the denatured
flours of which the greater majority of all
breads, rolls, cakes, cookies, crackers, muffins
and biscuits are made. These are the denatured
grains which compose most cooked and cold
cereals. The Yogi has no use for these products
which he considers not only without food value
but harmful. (I am limiting the enumeration of
the "harmful" possibilities of denatured foods
in this book; my primary objective is to con-

trast the low with the high life-force foods in each of the categories.)

Whole grains provide protein, vitamins and minerals in significant amounts. But they must be *whole grains*—unrefined, unbleached, without additives, and preferably *stone ground*. Fortunately, whole grain products, and also the whole grain flour from which you can make your own breads, rolls, and pastries, are more easily obtained than the pure foods in our other categories. Many markets stock at least one whole grain bread and the whole grain flours. Incidentally, be careful about the term "whole wheat" as it appears on the wrappers of many bakery products. Most whole wheat flour is processed. It is *whole grains* (wheat or otherwise) that we want.

Whole grain cereals (cracked wheat, buckwheat, hominy grits, groats, cornmeal) are available in markets and health food stores. These can be served as breakfast foods several times each week with fruits, a natural sweetener and milk or yogurt. Children should be encouraged to eat these whole grain products and discouraged from consuming the refined cold cereals which some nutritionists have labeled "sugared cardboard." Also, I can no longer find one of these processed cold cereals that does not also contain BHA.

Refined, polished white rice bears the same relationship to brown (whole) rice as refined flour does to the whole grain products. The polishing process which makes the rice white removes the all-important life-force germ and the layers immediately surrounding it. Consequently only brown (whole) rice should be used. In addition to the usual uses of rice, brown rice makes an excellent breakfast food and is especially good in cold weather.

The rice polishings as well as the wheat germ removed in processing are, of course, very high in vitamins. Fortunately, they are both available in package form. In addition to being excellent food supplements they lend a delicious flavor to many dishes and should be used as indicated in our recipes.

SUGAR

Sugar refining is that process which extracts the sugar from the cane or beet, *separating it from those elements which permit its proper digestion and assimilation*. As such, it becomes an extremely negative substance. Refined sugar kills life-force; it depletes the B vitamins, destroys the body's mineral relationships, enervates, produces irritability, obesity and restlessness. It is directly or indirectly responsible for more illness than can be listed on this page. The Yoga student avoids refined sugar in any and all forms. Also avoided are all low-calorie, coal tar "sugar substitutes," such as saccharin. (Mercifully, the cyclamates have now been at least partially banned by the government.)

Here are the sources of sugar in order of their nutritional preference:

Fresh fruits

Dried fruits (encourage these as between-meals snacks and substitutes for candy. Addiction to candy can result from its quick raising of the blood sugar level.)

Molasses (very rich in iron)

Maple sugar

Cane sugar (derived from chewing the cane stalks)

Beet sugar . (derived from eating the whole beet)

Honey (make certain it's uncooked and unbleached)

Carob (St. John's Bread; use the powder as described under "Legumes" or eat the pod)

Raw sugar

Brown sugar (just a little better than refined white sugar)

FEEDING YOUR FAMILY

Many students of Yoga are wives and mothers, responsible for feeding their families. Naturally, we believe that the Yoga nutrition program outlines the most truly nourishing way of eating, regardless of whether or not one is a Yoga student, and we know that many mothers will recognize the value of feeding their families, especially their children, according to its principles.

The transition from the usual processed food diet to that of natural foods must be made subtly with respect to your family, so that no hostility is generated. Most of the cereals, bakery products, vegetable dishes and natural sources of sugar that we have suggested can be substituted immediately since, in almost every case, these will prove more flavorful than the processed, denatured foods and cause no sense of deprivation. The reduction of flesh foods, pastas, desserts and other items may have to be accomplished gradually. Don't discuss this nutrition program with your family; just make the substitutions judiciously. If you are questioned about the new or different foods you are serving, it is best to answer in terms of "new flavors and recipes" rather than in terms of health, i.e. "This is good for you." If you eliminate meats and processed foods from your own diet but find it impossible to do so with your family, make a graceful excuse for yourself. You might say that you want to eat lightly or that you are watching your weight. At times, it may be necessary to prepare one entrée for yourself and another for the family. More work is involved but Yoga students understand the necessity of it.

I have four growing children of my own and I know the problems that can arise. If you are dedicated, you will quickly learn how to handle the various situations. I suggest that you never wholly deny your children the foods they ask for or crave. Simply *substitute*, gradually, wherever and whenever you can. The point is never to arouse hostility toward the program.

A word about babies: With the use of a blender, an infinite number of natural food combinations can be prepared for the infant and younger child without ever having to feed them denatured, processed foods.

SOCIAL DINING

You will be hard put to find more than a few dishes in any restaurant that conform to our principles. When you dine out, salads, vegetables, and fruits are your best bets. Eating a few dried fruits or other healthful snacks *before* you leave for the restaurant may be a good idea because it will diminish your appetite and you will find the lighter foods suggested above satisfying. When you are dining at a social or business affair, you will simply have to use your judgment.

Unless you are among the most sympathetic of friends, *I urge you not to discuss any aspect of your Yoga nutrition program.* If you ever refuse to eat a food that is served to you, do so with a graceful excuse. It is better to eat what is served than to be drawn into a discussion of your diet. Such discussions deplete life-force and often promote an unconscious hostility on the part of your listeners.

When you are entertaining or serving dinner to guests in your home you must compromise accordingly. If meat is expected, you'll have to serve it. However, many of our natural food recipes can be considered gourmet dishes and when you serve them your guests may be tasting the real flavors of fruits, vegetables, bread, etc. for the first time. Also remember that there are dozens of blender fruit drinks for light refreshments. My personal guests always find such drinks a welcome treat.

Incidentally, all larger cities now have many excellent health restaurants that conform to our principles. The number of such restaurants, even in smaller communities, is increasing at a rapid rate because more and more people are learning about the value of natural foods. Dining in such places can be a delightful experience, especially if the chef is imaginative; you will encounter combinations of foods and methods of preparation that will broaden your own cooking perspective.

YOGA NUTRITION AND WEIGHT CONTROL

Just as the practice of the Yoga exercises is designed to eliminate negative patterns of the body, and the meditation techniques are undertaken to liberate the mind, so will adherence to the principles of Yoga nutrition eventually free the student from those eating habits that result in excess weight.

When denatured foods are decreased and natural foods are substituted, the taste buds gradually lose their need for the various spices, seasonings, and sweeteners that are the chief attraction of the denatured foods. In this manner, Yoga students have experienced a loss of desire for the very foods that cause excess pounds. It is unnecessary to develop a weight regulation program apart from or as a special aspect of Yoga nutrition. With very few exceptions, one who follows the principles of our program cannot help but attain and maintain his correct weight!

Fasting

Before beginning the Yoga nutrition program it is often advantageous to fast for one or two days. Fasting means complete abstinence from food, drinking only water when thirsty. A short fast will act to cleanse the body and purify the taste buds. Then the natural flavors of unprocessed foods can be appreciated. If total abstinence seems too extreme, a more moderate fresh fruit juice fast can be undertaken for several days.

WHERE TO BUY
NATURAL FOODS

From the number of times the words "health food stores" have appeared in the preceding pages you may be led to conclude that the author has extensive holdings in the health food companies. Such is not the case. The simple fact is: There are vital foods that should be consumed in an unadulterated state and the business of the health food stores is to supply these products. Cereals, bakery and dairy products, fairly fresh fruit and vegetable juices, unsalted nuts and nut butters, unsulphured dried fruits, and often organic produce are available in these stores. There are smaller farms where organic fruits, vegetables and fertilized eggs can be obtained. A few inquiries should reveal their locations. Certain dairy companies will deliver raw milk, raw cream and butter. Many bakeries are beginning to make whole grain products. Fresh spring water is delivered by the water bottling companies. When organic produce is unavailable, fresh and frozen produce (to be very thoroughly soaked, washed and peeled if necessary) will be satisfactory. Whole grain flour and some bakery products, legumes, natural sugars, cheeses that conform to our principles, and spring water can be found in most larger markets. The growing demand for unprocessed foods is beginning to increase the sources of supply. We might note here that the case against the agents used in denaturing foods is now growing. Some of the chemical additives and pesticides have recently been cited by the FDA and we must hope that in the near future this agency will seriously investigate dozens of preservatives, flavorings, colorings, etc. that many nutritionists consider highly questionable. The day may come when the supermarkets will be stocked with an abundance of natural foods and denatured items will be the exception. But for the present you must develop your own sources of natural foods.

Remember: *before you buy, read the labels!*

Note: If you are under the care of a physician consult him before undertaking the Yoga Nutrition program.

II
RECIPES

**All recipes make 5–6 servings
unless otherwise indicated.**

SUGGESTED APPLIANCES AND UTENSILS

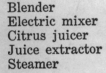

Blender
Electric mixer
Citrus juicer
Juice extractor
Steamer

Yogurt incubator
Food grinder
Nut mill
Shredder and grater

Heat-resistant casseroles (glass or stoneware)
Porcelain-coated cast iron pans (with tight-fitting lids)
Stainless steel pans (with tight-fitting lids)
Soup kettle (porcelain over steel)
Loaf, pie and cake pans (glass or steel)
Burner pad (metal or asbestos)

We advise against the use of all aluminum utensils. Because of the softness of the compound, aluminum can dissolve into food and be ingested.

TABLE OF EQUIVALENTS

2 tablespoons	=	1/8 cup
4 "	=	1/4 "
6 "	=	1/3 "
8 "	=	1/2 "
12 "	=	3/4 "
16 "	=	1 "

2 tablespoons	=	1 ounce
3 teaspoons	=	1 tablespoon

1 pint	=	2 cups
2 pints	=	1 quart
4 cups	=	1 quart
4 quarts	=	1 gallon

4 cups flour	=	1 pound
2¾ cups raw sugar	=	1 pound

1 pound shelled fresh peas	=	1 cup

1 large lemon	=	1/4 cup juice
1 medium orange	=	1/2 cup juice

SUBSTITUTIONS

You will find that certain of your favorite recipes which call for adulterated ingredients can be improved both in healthfulness and flavor by making substitutions from our various groups of pure, unprocessed foods.

Here, for example, are a few possibilities:

For	Substitute
1 oz. chocolate	4 tablespoons carob
1 cup white sugar	1⅓ cups raw sugar
	or
	1½ cups honey
1 cup white flour	⅞ cup whole wheat pastry flour

We encourage you to experiment with such substitutions.

BEVERAGES

OASIS SHAKE

1 small banana
1 heaping tablespoon
   dates (pitted and
   chopped)
1 level tablespoon
   sesame protein
   powder (available
   in health food
   stores)

¼ cup coconut milk
   (see this section)
1 cup milk

Place all ingredients in blender and blend well.
Serve at once or refrigerate and serve when
thoroughly chilled. Makes 2 cups.

CAROB HONEY SHAKE

1 tablespoon carob
   powder *
1 tablespoon sesame
   protein powder *

1 tablespoon honey
½ small banana
1 cup milk

Place all ingredients in blender and blend well.
Serve at once or refrigerate and serve when
thoroughly chilled.

* Available in most health food stores. Makes 1½
cups.

COCONUT MILK

Remove the liquid from coconut by punctur-
ing two of the three soft eyes and pouring the
coconut water into a container. Then open coconut by tapping sharply around the middle with
a hammer.

Grate 2 cups of the coconut meat in blender
or by hand. Pour 1 cup boiling water over coconut and let stand 30 minutes. Strain through
sieve and press out all liquid. Add original coconut water from container to mixture. Stir. Delicious in blender drinks, sauces and puddings.
Can be frozen.

Grated coconut meat has many uses, some of
which are indicated in this book.

GRAPE APPLE DRINK

½ cup grape juice
1 cup apple juice
2 teaspoons brewer's
   yeast *

1 teaspoon yogurt
¼ cup raisins

Blend in blender. Makes 2 cups.

* An excellent natural source of the B-complex vitamins. It is a powder, available in package form.

PINEAPPLE DRINK

1½ cups pineapple
    juice
1 ripe banana
1 tablespoon yogurt

2 teaspoons wheat
    germ powder *
1 teaspoon sunflower
    meal *

Blend in blender. Makes 2 cups.

   * Available in health food stores. Discussed previously.

FRUIT JUICE DRINK

¼ cup papaya juice
¼ cup orange juice

¼ cup pineapple juice
¼ cup coconut milk

Mix or blend. Makes 1 cup.

DATE NUT SHAKE

1 cup milk
½ cup dates (pitted)
1 tablespoon nut
    butter

1 tablespoon carob
    powder

Blend in blender. Makes 2 cups.

CAROB DRINK

1 cup milk
1 tablespoon carob
    powder
1 egg yolk

1 teaspoon wheat germ
    powder
1 drop pure vanilla
    extract

Blend in blender. Makes 1 cup.

APPLE JUICE DRINK

1 cup apple juice
1 tablespoon yogurt
1–2 teaspoons brewer's
    yeast

1 drop pure vanilla
    extract

Blend or mix well. Makes 1 cup.

WEIGHT GAINING DRINK

1 cup orange juice
1 teaspoon safflower oil
1 tablespoon carrot ice
    cream (see
    Desserts)

1 egg
1 tablespoon brewer's
    yeast
1 teaspoon cashew nut
    butter

Blend in blender. Makes 2 cups.

PINEAPPLE CARROT DRINK

½ cup pineapple juice
½ cup carrot juice
1 teaspoon lemon juice

1 teaspoon shredded
    coconut
2 teaspoons brewer's
    yeast

Blend in blender. Makes 1 cup.

CAROB MILK DRINK

2 cups milk
2 tablespoons carob
    powder
1 tablespoon honey or
    molasses

1 banana
1 tablespoon nut
    butter

Blend in blender. Makes 3 cups.

POTASSIUM (VEGETABLE) DRINK

¼ cup parsley juice
¼ cup carrot juice
¼ cup celery juice

¼ cup watercress
¼ cup spinach

Mix or blend. Makes 2 cups.

DATE MILK

1 cup milk
3 dates (chopped)
1 tablespoon coconut
    (shredded)

1 teaspoon wheat germ
    powder
1 teaspoon safflower oil

Blend in blender. Makes 1 cup.

GRAPE JUICE DRINK

1 cup grape juice
1 tablespoon brewer's
  yeast
1 tablespoon sunflower
  meal

1 tablespoon yogurt
1 teaspoon carob
  powder

Blend in blender. Makes 1½ cups.

VEGETABLE JUICE DRINK I

⅓ cup carrot juice
⅓ cup celery juice

⅓ cup tomato juice
1 tablespoon brewer's
  yeast

Mix well or blend in blender. Makes 1 cup.

VEGETABLE JUICE DRINK II

⅓ cup beet juice
⅓ cup cucumber juice

⅓ cup carrot juice
1 tablespoon brewer's
  yeast

Mix well or blend in blender. Makes 1 cup.

FRUIT JUICE-EGG DRINK

½ cup orange juice
½ cup papaya juice

1 egg
1 teaspoon honey

Mix or blend in blender. Makes 1½ cups.

VEGETABLE-FRUIT JUICE DRINK

½ cup carrot juice
½ cup papaya or
  coconut juice

1 banana
1 tablespoon wheat
  germ
2 dates (pitted)

Mix well or blend in blender. Makes 2 cups.

SALAD IN A GLASS

3 cups tomato juice   ½ stalk celery (sliced)
2 tomatoes (sliced)   1 green onion (sliced)
1 slice green pepper   3 sprigs fresh parsley
½ cucumber (sliced)

Put into blender container and liquefy. Makes
4–5 cups.

HOLIDAY PUNCH

1 qt. apple cider   ½ cup honey
Juice of 6 oranges   Orange slices studded
3 cups cranberry juice   with cloves
¼ cup lemon juice   Cinnamon bark sticks

Mix all liquids and honey. Serve chilled from
punchbowl with orange slices floating on top, or
heat and serve in mugs with cinnamon stick.
Makes 10 servings.

HERB TEAS

Place three to five teaspoonfuls of fresh or
dry herbs in a preheated china or pottery teapot. Bring water to a rolling boil and pour into
teapot. Steep about 5 minutes until tea is desired strength. Some delicious tea herbs are:

Alfalfa leaves   Hyssop
Camomile blossoms   Oat straw
Sarsparilla   Mint
Catnip   Parsley
Linden blossoms   Lavender blossoms
Rose hips   Sassafras
Comfrey   Fenugreek

Herbs can also be mixed in different combinations.

COOL TEAS

Place 4 teaspoonfuls of favorite herb or combination of herbs in a quart container. Fill container with spring or distilled water. Let stand until tea is desired strength, then strain and cool. Serve with honey, lemon, and sprig of mint.

CARROT MILK DRINK

½ cup carrot juice
½ cup milk
¼ cup almonds
  (chopped)

2 teaspoons wheat
  germ powder

Blend. Makes 1 cup.

PINEAPPLE COCONUT DRINK

½ cup coconut milk
½ cup pineapple juice

1 teaspoon powdered
  wheat germ
1 tablespoon yogurt

Blend or mix well. Makes 1 cup.

TOMATO DRINK

1 cup tomato juice
1 teaspoon parsley
  (chopped)

1 teaspoon lemon juice
2 teaspoons brewer's
  yeast

Blend. Makes 1 cup.

CARROT COCONUT DRINK

½ cup carrot juice
¼ cup celery juice
¼ cup coconut milk

1 teaspoon parsley
  (chopped)
1 teaspoon brewer's
  yeast

Blend. Makes 1 cup.

VEGETABLE DRINK

½ cup tomato juice
¼ cup celery juice
¼ cup carrot juice
¼ bunch water cress (chopped)

1 teaspoon parsley (chopped)
1 teaspoon lemon juice
2 teaspoons brewer's yeast

Blend. Makes 2 cups.

FRUIT MILK DRINK

½ cup raw or nonfat milk
½ cup any fruit juice

½ teaspoon honey (or more if desired)

Mix or blend. Makes 1 cup.

ENERGY DRINK

½ cup prune juice
½ cup apple juice
1 teaspoon nut butter

1 teaspoon yogurt
1 teaspoon soy, sesame or safflower oil

Blend. Makes 1½ cups.

APPETIZERS & SANDWICHES

HOMEMADE CREAM CHEESE

Keep 1 quart fresh cream at room temperature for 24 hours, or until it sours. Pour sour cream into clean cheese cloth bag. Suspend over bowl to catch dripping water. Let drain completely before taking it down. Mold solid cheese into small cakes. Keep refrigerated.

SESAME WHEAT CRACKERS

1 cup whole wheat
   flour
¼ teaspoon salt

¼ cup oil
2 tablespoons ice water

Sift flour and salt into oil. Mix and add water little by little until dough is like piecrust. Avoid handling more than absolutely necessary. Chill. Roll very thin and cut shapes with cookie cutter. Place on oiled cookie sheet and sprinkle with sesame seeds. Bake at 350°F. for 10 minutes.

MINERAL-RICH POTATO CURLS

Scrub raw potatoes with stiff brush under running water. Cut off thick slices of peelings. Brown these peelings in margarine or oil in a heavy skillet until curled and cooked.

Leftover potato centers are wonderful dough conditioners for bread making. Just boil and put through blender with water they were cooked in and use in place of plain water. Potato water improves the flavor of all baked goods.

FRUIT BUTTER

7–8 apples (peeled and cored) *
½ cup honey
Mace to taste
Cinnamon to taste
Cloves to taste
Ginger to taste

Slice apples into saucepan, add honey, spices and water to cover. Bring to boil, reduce heat and simmer 3–4 hours. Stir occasionally. Butter will be done when apples are a thick paste and a brown color. Blend in blender if a smoother consistency is desired.

* Other fruits may be used: peaches, plums, apricots, nectarines.

NUT BUTTER

1–2 tablespoons oil (sesame, soy)
Raw nuts *

If a blender is used, simply put nuts and amount of oil necessary into container and blend at a high speed until mixture becomes a thick paste. Some nuts, such as peanuts or cashews, will need little or no oil.

* Nut butters can be made from pignolias, almonds, walnuts, cashews, peanuts, filberts, Brazil nuts.

FRUIT-NUT BUTTER

1½ cup cashews   ½ cup sesame seeds
½ cup raisins

Grind or blend cashews. Chop raisins and add to nuts. Add sesame seeds. Blend well.

MELTED NATURAL CHEDDAR
SPECIAL SANDWICH

Cut two slices of whole wheat or rye bread in half. Place the four pieces on a toasting pan or baking sheet. Cover each piece with grated cheddar cheese. Sprinkle with a combination of a few hulled sunflower seeds, pumpkin seeds, and sesame seeds. Add a small amount of finely-chopped green onion. Toast until cheese melts and serve. Garnish with fresh lettuce, cucumber, tomato, carrot and parsley.

CREAM CHEESE SANDWICH

On two slices of whole wheat raisin bread, spread a generous amount of cream cheese. On one slice, sprinkle with chopped walnuts and on the other pitted chopped dates. Combine the two slices and cut sandwich in half, or in fourths as a party snack. Garnish with slices of apple and banana.

CUCUMBER TOMATO SANDWICH

Place a lettuce leaf on whole wheat or rye bread. On this place a layer of thinly sliced cucumber, then a layer of thinly sliced tomato and finish with a paper-thin slice of onion. Add another slice of bread spread with homemade mayonnaise or margarine.

AVOCADO SANDWICH

1 ripe avocado
¼ teaspoon fresh
   lemon juice
1 teaspoon green
   onions
   (finely chopped)

⅛ teaspoon dill weed
⅛ teaspoon sea salt
¼ teaspoon parsley
   (chopped)

Peel and mash avocado. Add other ingredients and blend together. Serve on wholesome whole grain bread with alfalfa sprouts.

NUT BUTTER SANDWICH

Spread two slices of whole wheat raisin bread with a generous amount of almond, cashew and peanut butters cambined. On one slice sprinkle pitted chopped dates, and on the other add banana slices. Combine the two slices and cut sandwich in half or fourths and serve as a party snack. Garnish with slices of fresh apple, pear, or other fruit.

SPREADS

(for sandwiches, hors d'oeuvres and appetizers)

FRUIT NUT BUTTER SPREAD

½ cup nut butter
   (your choice)

3 tablespoons raisins
½ peeled orange

Blend in blender. Add sufficient yogurt or orange juice to make mixture spreadable.

DATE–NUT SPREAD

1 cup dates

½ cup nuts
   (your choice)

Blend in blender. Add sufficient yogurt to make mixture spreadable.

CARROT HONEY SPREAD

3 sliced carrots   **1 tablespoon honey**

Blend in blender. Add sufficient yogurt to make mixture spreadable.

NUT CREAM CHEESE SPREAD

¼ cup ground walnuts   **3 oz. cream cheese**

Blend in blender with sufficient yogurt to make spreadable.

CHIVE SPREAD

1 tablespoon chives or   **4 tablespoons chopped**
scallions (chopped)   **black olives**
                                    3 oz. cream cheese

Blend olives with cream cheese. Add chives to mixture.

GARBANZO-SESAME SPREAD

2 cups garbanzo beans (cooked) (also called chick peas or ceci beans)

To cook, soak overnight ¾ cup beans in water to cover. Rinse, cover with water, and cook over medium heat approximately 2 hours or until soft enough to mash.

1 lb. Tahini (sesame seed butter, available in most health food stores. If unavailable, grind ¾ cup sesame seed in blender, a small amount at a time. To this meal, add enough sesame oil to make a thick paste)
¼ cup olive oil
2 tablespoons green onion (finely chopped)
2 tablespoons parsley (chopped)
2 teaspoons sea salt

Mash cooked garbanzo beans. Add Tahini and blend well. Add other ingredients and serve.

Excellent cold after being refrigerated. Serve on wholesome whole grain bread with alfalfa sprouts.

HORS D'OEUVRES

A tray of varied cheese is always tantalizing party fare. Such a tray might include:

Cheddar	Gruyère Swiss
Muenster	Jack

A pleasant complement to a cheese tray is another platter with finger-sized slices of fresh fruit or whole fruit such as:

Crisp apple	Stuffed prunes
Papaya	Cold grapes
Pineapple spears	Peaches

It's always best to make your own, but many whole grain crackers without preservatives are available. The sesame seed variety is especially delicious. Pumpernickel, rye and most whole grain breads are tasty sliced very thin and then each slice cut in quarters or thirds. On each piece a filling or spread can be arranged:

Cheddar cheese and grated apple
Avocado, chives, and lemon juice
Cream cheese and alfalfa sprouts
Artichoke hearts blended with olive oil
    and lemon
Cheddar cheese topped with black olive
See also spreads and nut butters

SOUPS

ONION SOUP

4 brown onions
(chopped)
1 stalk celery with
leaves (chopped)
4 tablespoons oil
2 cups stock (water in
which vegetables
were cooked, beans
were soaked, or
plain water)

2 cups tomato juice
Vegetable salt to taste
Garlic powder to taste
1½ thick slices whole
wheat bread
Margarine
Parmesan cheese

Sauté onions and celery in oil until lightly browned. Add stock, juice and seasonings. Cover and simmer 15 minutes. Cut bread in fourths, spread each piece with margarine, sprinkle with parmesan cheese and place under broiler to brown. Float one piece of cheese bread in each bowl of soup.

MINESTRONE

1 cup beans (pea,
    marrow or navy,
    soaked overnight)
6 cups water
¼ cup olive oil
1 clove garlic (minced)
2 tablespoons parsley
2 tablespoons celery
1 cup cabbage
    (chopped)

½ cup vegetable or
    whole wheat
    macaroni
3 cups tomato juice or
    stock
¼ teaspoon oregano
Parmesan cheese
Vegetable salt to taste

Simmer beans in water they were soaked in until tender. Brown onion, garlic and celery in oil. Add beans, water and remaining ingredients. Simmer 30–40 minutes. Top with parmesan cheese and serve.

LENTIL SOUP

1 onion (chopped)
4 tablespoons olive oil
2 cloves garlic
    (minced)
2–3 stalks celery with
    tops (chopped)
2 tomatoes (chopped)
2–3 carrots (chopped)

2 cups lentils
1 tablespoon lemon
    juice
Savory
Thyme
Parsley
Oregano

Sauté onion in olive oil; reduce heat and add garlic, cook a few minutes. Chop vegetables by hand or with water in blender. Add chopped vegetables, 1½ qts. water and lentils. Bring to boil, then lower heat and simmer slowly for about 2 hours until lentils are tender. Serve as is with whole lentils or blend some and return to pot for thicker stock.

PUERTO RICAN BLACK BEAN SOUP

1 lb. black beans
4 cloves garlic
½ tablespoon
   vegetable salt
1½ teaspoons cumin
1½ teaspoons oregano

5 tablespoons olive oil
2 onions (chopped)
2 green peppers
   (chopped and
   seeded)

Soak beans in water to cover, overnight. Add water to make two quarts and cook until tender. Put garlic, salt and herbs in a mortar and crush. Sauté vegetables in oil until transparent. Add garlic mixture and a tablespoon or two of water and simmer a few minutes. Add this mixture to beans and simmer 30 minutes.

SPLIT PEA SOUP

1 cup split peas
1 qt. water
1 large onion
   (chopped)
2 stalks celery
   (chopped)
4 carrots (chopped)

¼ cup parsley
1 teaspoon soy or olive
   oil or margarine
1 teaspoon oregano
1 teaspoon basil
Vegetable salt to taste

Combine all ingredients. Bring to boil, then reduce heat and simmer 2 hours. If smoother consistency is desired, blend in blender.

FRESH PEA SOUP

3 cups shelled peas
2 cups water
¼ cup green onions
   (chopped)
3 tablespoons whole
   wheat flour

3 tablespoons
   margarine
   (melted)
3 cups milk
Chives or mint
   (chopped)

Cook peas in water until tender. Blend peas, cooking liquid and onions in blender. Melt margarine, stir in flour, and cook gently 3–4 minutes. Slowly stir in milk and cook until it thickens. Add the puréed peas and blend well. Chill and sprinkle fresh chives or mint on top.

YOGURT SOUP

1 pt. yogurt
3 cucumbers (sliced)
3 tablespoons soy oil
3 tablespoons lemon
    juice
½ teaspoon dill

1 clove garlic
    (minced)
½ teaspoon dill seeds
1 tablespoon mint
1 teaspoon lemon rind
    (grated)

Place all ingredients in blender container and blend until smooth. Chill and garnish with fresh dill.

VEGETABLE SOUP

Soy sauce   yeast

1 large onion
    (chopped)
3 fresh tomatoes
    (cut up)
3 stalks celery with
    tops
3 carrots (sliced)
2 cups green beans
    (chopped)

1 Italian squash (cut
    in cubes)
1 potato (cut in cubes)
2 cloves garlic
    (minced)
4 tablespoons olive oil
1 bay leaf
Marjoram to taste,
    parsley

Chop onion and brown lightly in oil. Add tomatoes and garlic. Simmer a few minutes. Add 1 quart of water and bring to boil. Add vegetables and herbs. Bring to simmer. Vegetable salt to taste. Cook until vegetables are tender.

BLENDER BORSCH

2 cups yogurt
1½ cups beets (cooked
    and sliced)

¼ lemon (seeded and
    peeled)
¼ teaspoon celery salt
¼ teaspoon onion salt

Put all ingredients in blender container and blend. Serve chilled topped with dollop of yogurt.

POTATO SOUP

4 lbs. potatoes
¼ cup margarine
1 onion (chopped)

1 teaspoon paprika
4 cups water
2 cups milk (scalded)
Celery salt

Sauté onions in margarine with paprika until onion is clear and tender. Add water and boil. Peel and slice potatoes and add to boiling water. Lower heat and cook mixture uncovered until potatoes are tender. Add milk and cook until potatoes are mushy. Blend for smoother consistency. Serve.

For an interesting variation: Stir ½ lb. grated Muenster cheese into hot soup just before serving. Salt to taste.

FRESH TOMATO PURÉE

6–8 ripe tomatoes
(peeled and
chopped)

1 tablespoon
margarine

Tomatoes are best when they are about 2 inches in diameter, deep red, and slightly heart-shaped. Place tomatoes in saucepan. Add margarine. Cook sauce until smooth, stirring often. If even smoother purée is desired, blend in blender.

BLENDER CREAM OF TOMATO SOUP

2 cups tomatoes
(stewed or puréed)
3 tablespoons whole
wheat flour

1 teaspoon soy flour
½ onion (chopped)
Vegetable salt to taste
1 quart milk

Place ingredients in blender and blend well. Pour into saucepan and simmer a few minutes, stirring well.

CREAM OF BROCCOLI SOUP

2 lbs. broccoli
1 onion (chopped)
1 large can evaporated
  milk

1 bay leaf
Vegetable salt to taste
Nutmeg to taste

Place washed broccoli in pot with onion and bay leaf. Cover with water, bring to boil and cook until tender. Drain. Save liquid and add water, if necessary, to make 2 cups. Put liquid and vegetables in blender container and blend. Put in saucepan and stir in milk. Add seasonings and reheat. Sprinkle chopped chives or sesame seeds on top.

GAZPACHO

3 cups tomato juice
3 tomatoes (peeled,
  seeded and diced)
1 cucumber (diced)
1 green pepper (finely
  chopped)
1 tablespoon parsley
  (chopped)

1 tablespoon cider
  vinegar
Juice of one lemon
Vegetable salt to taste
1 clove garlic
  (mashed)

Mix all ingredients well and chill. Serve with garnish of sliced avocado.

BARLEY SOUP

2 onions (chopped)
4 carrots (chopped)
1 turnip (chopped)
4 tablespoons
  margarine

1 cup pearl barley
7 cups water
Parsley
Vegetable salt to taste

Sauté the onions, carrots and turnip in margarine until transparent and slightly browned. Add water, bring to boil, then add barley. Cover and simmer gently for 2 hours. Thin with warm milk if necessary. Garnish with chopped parsley.

STRACCIATELLA

6 cups stock
2 bunches spinach
2 eggs (beaten)
¼ cup whole wheat bread crumbs
¼ cup Parmesan cheese (grated)

Simmer stock and add torn up spinach. Simmer for 3 minutes. Mix together the eggs, crumbs and cheese. Bring stock to a boil and stir in egg mixture. Serve immediately.

CABBAGE AND POTATO SOUP

3 potatoes
1 onion (chopped)
½ lb. cabbage (finely shredded)
½ cup olive oil or margarine
1 qt. water
Vegetable salt to taste

Place water, onion and vegetable salt in a soup kettle and bring to a boil. Peel and slice potatoes, add them to liquid and cook until tender. Force potatoes through ricer and return to water. Add cabbage to potatoes, with oil, and cook 3–4 minutes.

CHEESE AND BLACK BREAD SOUP

4 cups milk
6 slices toasted black bread (pumpernickel or rye)
½ lb. grated Gruyère Swiss cheese
¼ cup butter
Dash of nutmeg

Place toast in each bowl and place on top of

toast a generous layer of cheese. Simmer milk and skim. Add nutmeg and margarine and pour around toast.

JACK O'LANTERN PUMPKIN SOUP

1 pumpkin, 10–12 inch diameter
3 cups toasted whole wheat bread crumbs

¾ lb. Gruyère Swiss cheese
Milk (as needed)
Vegetable salt to taste
Freshly ground nutmeg

Cut lid in pumpkin, Jack O'Lantern style. Remove seeds and fibrous membranes. Alternate layers of bread crumbs and sliced cheese. Season. Pour in milk to within 1 inch of top of pumpkin. Replace lid and bake entire pumpkin at 350°F. approximately 1 hour, until pumpkin is tender. Check midway during cooking and add more milk if necessary. Serve soup in pumpkin, scooping bits of pumpkin meat with soup.

SALADS
(Vegetable & Fruit)

PHIL'S LUNCH SALAD BOWL

1 head Boston lettuce
Oak leaf lettuce
Celery (thinly sliced)
Alfalfa sprouts
Zucchini or Italian
   squash (thinly
   sliced)

2 tablespoons pumpkin
   seeds
2 tablespoons
   sunflower seeds

Toss all ingredients together with natural herb
dressing.

ROMAINE SALAD

1 head Romaine
   lettuce
¼ cup olive oil
¼ cup parmesan
   cheese

Vegetable salt
¼ cup lemon juice
1 cup whole wheat
   croutons

Toss one head crisp fresh romaine lettuce (leaves broken into bite-size pieces) with above ingredients, in the order given.

BROCCOLI SALAD

3 cups fresh broccoli
   buds (steamed
   lightly)
1 cup cherry tomatoes
   (cut in half)

½ Bermuda onion
   (sliced thinly)
1 teaspoon fresh basil
Vegetable salt to taste

Combine all ingredients, and toss well with lemon juice and olive oil dressing.

RAW STRING BEAN SALAD

1 head iceberg
   lettuce

1 lb. tender, young
   green string beans
   (slivered)

Combine string beans with lettuce and serve with French, or natural herb dressing.

GREEN BEAN SALAD

2 cups crisp, raw green
   string beans
3 bunches spinach
2 tomatoes (sliced)

½ Bermuda onion
   (thinly sliced)
¼ head Boston lettuce

Remove strings and break each bean into 3 or 4 pieces. Break up spinach and lettuce, mix all ingredients together, and toss with kelp or herb dressing.

BEAN SPROUT SALAD

¼ lb. mung bean
   sprouts
Celery
Caraway seeds

Pecans or walnuts
Honey
Lemon juice

Chop celery and nuts. Mix with bean sprouts.
Mix in enough caraway seeds to add a delicate
flavor. Add honey and lemon to taste. Serve on
lettuce.

LENTIL SPROUT SALAD

2 bunches fresh
   spinach (torn into
   pieces)
1 large red apple,
   unpeeled (cored,
   quartered and
   sliced thinly)
1 cup lentil sprouts

½ Bermuda onion
   (sliced thinly)
3 tablespoons olive oil
2 tablespoons lemon
   juice
1 teaspoon Fines
   Herbes *
Vegetable salt to taste

Toss spinach, apple, sprouts and onion together.
Mix oil, vinegar, lemon juice, herbs and salt together. Pour over salad, and toss well. Also
delicious with Kelp Dressing (see Salad Dressings).

* See Natural Herb Dressing under Salad Dressings.

SPROUTED WHEAT SALAD

1½ cups sprouted
   wheat
½ cup green onion
   (chopped)

½ cup celery
   (chopped)
2 avocados

Cube avocado and toss with sprouts, onions and
celery. Serve on crisp lettuce leaves with lemon
juice dressing.

GREEK SALAD

1 head romaine or
   iceberg lettuce
2 tomatoes
5 green onions
15 Greek olives (pitted
   and cut in half)
10 radishes (sliced)

¼ lb. Feta cheese
   (available at
   markets selling
   Mediterranean
   products
¼ teaspoon oregano

Dressing:
¼ cup lemon juice
¼ cup olive oil
Vegetable salt

Wash greens thoroughly and break into salad
bowl. Cut tomatoes in wedges and dice green
onions. Add olives and radishes. Crumble Feta
cheese over salad, pour on salad dressing and
toss well.

SPINACH SALAD

1 lb. raw, crisp spinach
1 clove garlic (minced)
1 onion (grated)
2 tablespoons lemon
   juice

7 tablespoons oil
Tomato wedges
3 hard cooked eggs
   (quartered)

Break up spinach. Blend garlic, onion, lemon
juice and oil together. Toss spinach and dressing. Garnish with tomatoes and eggs.

RAW SPINACH SALAD

2 cups raw spinach
4 ripe tomatoes

½ Bermuda onion

Cut up tomatoes, break spinach, and shave
onion in paper-thin slices. Serve on lettuce
leaves with lemon juice dressing.

EGYPTIAN SALAD

4 cucumbers
½ teaspoon fresh
   garlic (finely
   chopped)
1 cup yogurt

1 teaspoon fresh dill
   (finely chopped)..
3 radishes (thinly
   sliced)

Peel cucumbers, cut in half lengthwise and slice fine. In a salad bowl blend garlic, yogurt and dill. Add cucumber and radish slices and toss well.

CUCUMBER SALAD

2–3 cucumbers
1 cup yogurt
3 tablespoons green
   onions (chopped)

3 tablespoons lemon
   juice
½ teaspoon dill weed

Combine, chill, and serve.

RAW PEA SALAD

1 cup fresh raw peas
2 cups carrots

1 green onion
1 cup sunflower seeds

Grate carrots, chop onion, add peas and sunflower seeds. Add preferred dressing.

KIDNEY, GARBANZO AND STRING BEAN SALAD

1½ cups kidney beans
   (cooked)
1½ cups garbanzo
   beans (cooked)
2 cups string beans
   (freshly steamed)
½ clove garlic
   (minced)

½ Bermuda or
   Spanish onion
   (chopped)
½ cup olive oil
½ cup red wine or
   cider vinegar
1 teaspoon basil
1 teaspoon oregano

Serve on lettuce leaves with tomato wedges.

BEET SALAD

Peel thin skin from young tender beets and grate them or use the finest cutter on the food chopper. Keep in refrigerator, and when ready to serve, use a dressing of lemon juice, honey and oil.

GUACAMOLE

Mash avocados (1 per person) in a bowl. Add finely chopped onion, a clove of garlic (pressed). Mix thoroughly with lemon juice and olive oil (1 or 2 teaspoons). Serve on lettuce with crisp wheat crackers.

COMBINATION SALAD

1 cucumber
2 tomatoes
1 green pepper
3 stalks of celery
1 bunch of washed
    spinach (chopped
    fine)

1 medium size head of
    lettuce
6–8 sprigs of
    watercress

Cut all ingredients fine and use a good quantity of lemon, oil and honey dressing.

EGGPLANT SALAD

½ eggplant
½ cauliflower
4 bunches of spinach
2 yellow squash

½ Bermuda onion
½ cup bean sprouts
¼ cup pumpkin seeds

Slice eggplant lengthwise 3–4 times, then cut these crosswise into thin (⅛ inch) slices. Slice cauliflower, squash and onion thinly. Break up spinach and mix together with sliced vegetables, sprouts and seeds. Toss with herb dressing.

DANDELION SALAD

1 clove garlic
1 lb. tender dandelion
   greens

¾ cup black olives
1 ripe tomato (cut in
   eighths)

Rub bowl with garlic. Add all ingredients, and toss with olive oil and lemon juice dressing.

LEEK SALAD

1 clove garlic
1 head Romaine lettuce
   (torn in pieces)
3 young, tender leeks
   (sliced)
1 tomato (sliced)

Chervil
Basil
3 tablespoons olive oil
2 tablespoons lemon
   juice

Thoroughly rub inside of wooden salad bowl with garlic clove. Add Romaine, leeks, tomato and herbs. Mix oil and lemon juice and pour over salad. Toss well.

COTTAGE CHEESE SALAD

4 radishes (sliced thin)
2 green onions (sliced
   thin)
¼ small cucumber
   (sliced thin)

1 cup mung bean
   sprouts
½ cup cottage cheese
½ cup yogurt

Mix vegetables and sprouts. Add cheese and yogurt.

HERB GARDEN COTTAGE CHEESE

1 lb. cottage cheese
¼ cup yogurt
¼ cup poppy seeds
¼ cup caraway seeds
¼ cup sesame seeds
Garlic powder
1 teaspoon chives
   (minced)

1 sprig of each
   (minced):
   marjoram
   basil
   thyme
   sage
   parsley and dill
Vegetable salt to taste

Blend all together and refrigerate for 1 hour or more before serving.

COLESLAW

6 tablespoons yogurt	1 tablespoon milk
2 tablespoons mayonnaise (make your own)	Vegetable salt Celery salt Dill
2 tablespoons yogurt	1 head cabbage (shredded)
2 tablespoons lemon juice	

Blend first five ingredients. Mix with cabbage and seasoning.

POTATO SALAD

2 lbs. potatoes	3 hard boiled eggs (sliced)
1 onion (sliced thinly)	¼ cup ripe olives (chopped)
1 cup mayonnaise	
6 tablespoons olive oil	
¼ cup cider vinegar	Vegetable salt to taste

Boil potatoes in skins until tender, peel and cut into thin slices or cubes. Combine warm potatoes with onion, salt, vinegar and oil. Add mayonnaise, olives, and all egg slices but four. Garnish with remaining egg slices.

AVOCADO ON THE HALF SHELL

Cut the fruit in half and remove the seed. Serve one-half to each person. Fill cavity with olive oil and lemon juice.

RAW VEGETABLE FINGER SALAD

Wash and slice into finger-sized sticks any or all of the following:

Broccoli
Carrots
Celery
Green onion
Zucchini
Cauliflower
Cucumbers
Eggplant

Turnip
Bermuda onion
Bell pepper
Radishes
Rutabaga
Potato
Whole cherry tomatoes

Dip in yogurt or guacamole.

INDIA NUT SALAD

2 cups nuts, pecans or
   walnuts (chopped)
8 pitted dates
   (chopped)
¼ cup coconut
   (shredded)

1 red apple, unpeeled
   (cored and sliced)
3 tablespoons raisins
1 head Boston lettuce
   (torn into pieces)

Combine all ingredients and toss with French
dressing.

FRESH FRUIT SALAD

1 cup bananas (sliced,
   tossed with lemon
   juice to prevent
   darkening)
1 cup strawberries
1 cup peaches

½ cup coconut
   (freshly grated)
¼ cup chopped nuts
   (almonds or
   pignolias)

Mix together. Add honey if needed.

PAPAYA PINEAPPLE SALAD

2 papayas
1 banana
½ pineapple

3 tablespoons lemon
   juice
4 tablespoons honey

Peel papayas, remove seeds and cut into chunks.
Reserve seeds for use in dressing. Peel banana
and pineapple, and cut into chunks. Mix all fruits

together. Serve with Papaya Seed dressing (see Salad Dressings).

PEAR SALAD

4 pears (marinated)   ½ pt. cottage cheese

Marinate pears (whole or halves) in French dressing. Make mound of cottage cheese on platter and place pears around the cheese as border. Pour the dressing over all.

CANTALOUPE CUP

Cut in half. Remove seeds. Fill with berries in season (any fruits in season may be used). Top with yogurt or sprinkle with honey or coconut.

APPLE SALAD

4 apples (grated)   ½ lb. almonds
¾ cup raisins   (ground)
                           Nutmeg to taste

Mix above ingredients and serve.

DRIED FRUIT SALAD

1 cup dates (chopped)   1 cup raisins
1 cup figs (chopped)   1 cup coconut (grated)

Mix ingredients together and toss with yogurt and honey.

WINTER SALAD

3 apples   10 pecans or walnuts
2 stalks celery   1 banana
¼ cup raisins

Chop all ingredients. Dress with mayonnaise and yogurt mixture (equal quantities of each).

TANGERINE WATERCRESS SALAD

2 bunches watercress
(well-chilled)
5–6 juicy tangerines
(peeled, seeded and
diced) or 3–4
oranges

Dressing:
¼ cup olive oil
2 teaspoons cider
vinegar
1 teaspoon lemon juice
1 teaspoon honey

Toss cleaned watercress with diced tangerines,
then toss with dressing.

WALDORF SALAD

2 cups tart, crisp
apples (diced)
1 cup celery (chopped)

½ cup pecans
½ cup seedless raisins

Mix with mayonnaise. Serve on crisp lettuce
leaves.

BLENDER CARROT SALAD

3 cups carrots (sliced)
½ cup seedless raisins

¾ cup fresh or frozen
pineapple chunks
⅓ cup mayonnaise

Place cut-up carrots in blender. Add water to
cover and chop at medium speed for 2 or 3
minutes. Drain off liquid and save for use in
soups or gravy. Add remaining ingredients and
toss well. Carrots can, of course, be grated by
hand.

WATERCRESS AND GRAPEFRUIT SALAD

Select 3 sweet grapefruits. Remove peel and
membranes, separate into sections and remove
seeds. Place a bunch or two of watercress,
broken up, in the bowl, add grapefruit sections
and toss with French dressing. Increase honey

slightly to compensate for tartness of grape-fruit.

ENDIVE AND ORANGE SALAD

Wash 2–3 Belgian endives and cut in half. Cut out thick stalk. Peel and slice thinly 2–3 oranges. Arrange endives and orange slices on plate on top of crisp lettuce, or fresh water-cress. Pour on a little French dressing.

SALAD DRESSINGS

NATURAL HERB DRESSING

⅔ cup lemon juice
   (freshly squeezed)
1⅓ cups pure olive oil
1 clove garlic
   (optional)

¼ teaspoon anise seed
¼ teaspoon dill weed
¼ teaspoon spearmint
¼ teaspoon tarragon
¼ teaspoon "Fines
   Herbes"

("Fines Herbes" are sold at most stores carrying a good selection of herbs and spices. If unavailable, it is an equal combination of sage, oregano, thyme, basil, marjoram and rosemary. Make your own.)

Crush garlic (if used). Crush anise seeds and add to garlic. Crush other herbs into fine pieces and add to oil and lemon juice. Shake well and use on any green salad. Refrigerate.

BLENDER HERB DRESSING

2 tablespoons lemon
    juice or cider
    vinegar
¼ cup watercress or
    spinach (chopped)
2 tablespoons green
    onions (chopped)

1 egg yolk
¼ cup oil
1 teaspoon honey
1 teaspoon savory
1 teaspoon parsley
1 teaspoon tarragon
1 teaspoon dill

Blend all ingredients in blender until smoothy mixed.

FRENCH DRESSING

¾ cup vegetable oil
¼ cup lemon juice
1–3 teaspoons honey

1 clove garlic
1 teaspoon vegetable
    salt

Mix together in covered jar and shake well.

KELP DRESSING

2 cups olive oil
½ teaspoon powdered
    kelp

Juice of 1 lemon
Vegetable salt to taste

Blend or shake well.

THOUSAND ISLAND DRESSING

1 cup olive oil
1 cup tomato purée
⅓ cup lemon juice

¼ onion (chopped
    fine)
¼ cup honey

Mix and shake in a covered jar.

SESAME SEED DRESSING

1 clove garlic (minced)
2 teaspoons sesame
    seed

½ cup olive oil
3 tablespoons lemon
    juice
Vegetable salt to taste

Sauté garlic, sesame seed and olive oil lightly. Cool and shake well with rest of ingredients.

TOMATO DRESSING

½ cup soy oil
¼ cup lemon juice

¼ cup tomato juice
Vegetable salt to taste

(If possible, make your own tomato juice in your vegetable juice extractor.)

Mix together in covered jar and shake well.

YOGURT DRESSING

1 cup plain yogurt
2 tablespoons lemon juice

½ teaspoon paprika
1 clove garlic (minced)
¼ onion (grated)

Beat above ingredients together thoroughly.

AVOCADO DRESSING

1 clove garlic (mashed)
1 green onion (chopped very fine)

1 ripe avocado (mashed)

Mix all above ingredients together, add a small amount of milk and mix well again.

MAYONNAISE

2 cups oil (safflower, soy, olive or sunflower)
2 egg yolks
4 tablespoons lemon juice

1–2 teaspoons honey
¼ teaspoon dry mustard
1 teaspoon vegetable salt

Measure oil into pitcher or another container that is easy to pour from. Combine the rest of the ingredients in blender container, or small mixer jar, and blend. Continue beating and drip oil into mixture slowly. If oil is added too fast, mayonnaise will not thicken. Stop adding oil when consistency is right, even if entire amount of oil is not used up.

PAPAYA SEED DRESSING

2 tablespoons fresh papaya seeds	½ cup honey
2 cups safflower oil	½ cup lemon juice
	Spearmint

Place all ingredients in blender container. Blend until seeds are ground up. Serve on fruits.

YOGURT FRUIT SALAD DRESSING

1 cup yogurt	2 tablespoons honey
2 tablespoons lemon juice	

Beat well.

COTTAGE CHEESE DRESSING

Place amount of cottage cheese needed in blender container and blend at high speed for 5 minutes.

ENTRÉES

RATATOUILLE

(Zucchini–Eggplant–Tomato Casserole)

1 medium-sized
  eggplant
3 zucchini
3 firm tomatoes
1 large onion
4–6 tablespoons olive
  oil

3 cloves garlic
Vegetable salt to taste
½ teaspoon oregano
Grated Parmesan
  cheese

Peel and cut both the eggplant and the zucchini into one and one-half inch cubes. Chop tomatoes coarsely; slice the onion lengthwise and set aside. Pour the olive oil into a large skillet and when it is hot, sauté the zucchini and eggplant until lightly browned. Remove from pan, lower heat and add the onions, tomatoes, garlic and oregano. Simmer until onions are limp. Place all ingredients in casserole, sprinkle with Parmesan, cover and bake at 300°F. for one hour.

MARINARA SAUCE

2 stalks celery
(chopped)
½ eggplant (diced)
½ bell pepper
(chopped)
1 onion (chopped)

1 clove garlic (minced)
½ teaspoon oregano
½ teaspoon basil
¼ cup olive oil
6–8 tomatoes
1 can tomato paste

Sauté everything except tomatoes. When vegetables are clear and limp, add tomatoes, chopped in blender, and tomato paste diluted with 1 cup of water. Simmer about 45 minutes and serve over artichoke or whole wheat spaghetti noodles. Sprinkle with Parmesan cheese.

WILD RICE AND MUSHROOMS

1 cup wild rice (raw)
2 cups water or
vegetable stock
½ lb. fresh
mushrooms
(sliced)
2 tablespoons oil

2 cups celery (finely
chopped)
1 onion (chopped)
1 green pepper
(chopped)
5 tablespoons olive oil
½ cup tomato juice

The night before, pour boiling stock or water over well-washed rice. The next day, liquid will be absorbed and rice ready to use. Sauté mushrooms in oil. In another skillet, sauté vegetables in olive oil until limp. Stir together with rice and mushrooms. Turn into oiled casserole and pour tomato juice over ingredients. Bake at 350°F. until liquid is absorbed.

MUSHROOM CASSEROLE

4 cups mushrooms
(sliced)
1 onion (minced)
1 teaspoon oregano

½ teaspoon rosemary
3 tablespoons brewers'
yeast
¼ cup water

Brown mushrooms and onions briefly in oil. Add

remaining ingredients. Turn into casserole. Cover. Bake at 350°F. for 20 minutes.

MUSHROOM BROWN RICE

6 cups cooked brown rice
1½ cups oil
¼ cup parsley (minced)
1 cup onion (chopped)
2 cups fresh mushrooms (sliced)
Vegetable salt to taste

Sauté onion in ½ cup oil; remove, then sauté mushrooms. Add remaining oil to cooked rice and toss lightly; add mushrooms and onions. Season with vegetable salt. Serve with parsley sprinkled over each serving.

RISOTTO

1 onion (chopped)
1 clove garlic (minced)
1 cup brown rice (raw)
2 cups water or vegetable stock
Pinch of saffron
½ teaspoon rosemary
3 tablespoons parsley (minced)
½ cup cheddar cheese (grated)

Sauté onion, garlic and rice in oil until golden brown. Pour in ½ of the stock and sprinkle in herbs and saffron. Cook gently, adding more stock as mixture dries out. When rice is tender and all liquid absorbed, sprinkle with cheese and mix until cheese is just melted.

BALKAN PILAF

2 large onions (chopped)
4 tablespoons olive oil
¼ cup chopped nuts (pignolia, almonds)
2 cups brown rice (raw)
¼ cup currants or raisins
2 tomatoes (sliced)
4 cups stock
1 teaspoon sage
1 teaspoon parsley
½ teaspoon allspice
Vegetable salt to taste

Sauté onions in oil until transparent. Stir in rice and nuts, and cook 5 minutes. Add remaining ingredients. Place tight-fitting lid on pan and cook over very low heat until all liquid is absorbed. Asbestos burner pad is helpful in this instance. Rice will be tender in 30–40 minutes.

SPINACH QUICHE

2 lbs. fresh spinach
2 tablespoons green onions (chopped)
3 tablespoons margarine
3 eggs (beaten)
1 cup yogurt

½ cup non-fat milk
½ teaspoon vegetable salt
½ teaspoon nutmeg
¼ cup Gruyère Swiss cheese (grated)

Line a 9-inch Quiche Lorraine dish with whole wheat pastry. (If dish not available, a pie pan will be adequate.)

Wash spinach well, removing stems and any bad parts. Plunge into boiling water for about 1 minute, drain very well and blot thoroughly with paper towels. Chop spinach, add onions and cook in 2 tablespoons margarine for 2–3 minutes until no liquid shows. Combine eggs, yogurt, cream and seasonings, beat well. Add spinach mixture and pour into crust. Sprinkle with cheese and dot with margarine. Bake at 375°F. for 25 minutes. Serve hot.

SPINACH AND MUSHROOMS

2 lbs. spinach
½ onion (chopped)
1¼ lbs. fresh mushrooms (sliced)

¼ cup water
3 tablespoons yogurt
Vegetable salt to taste
4–5 cups cooked brown rice

Wash spinach well and steam in its own moisture until just tender. Sauté onions and sliced

106

mushrooms in margarine until lightly browned. Drain spinach, saving water, if any. Chop spinach and cook with mushrooms just a few minutes. Add the spinach liquid or water, stir, and then add the yogurt. Heat through and add vegetable salt. Serve on rice.

SPINACH FAR EAST

2 pounds spinach (or
    beet tops), steamed
½ cup oil

Juice of 1 lemon
1 onion (minced)
½ cup sesame seeds

Mix together. Serve cold.

GREEK SPINACH PIE

½ lb. Phyllo pastry
    (available at
    Mediterranean
    delicatessens and
    shops)
1½ lbs. Feta cheese
2 lbs. spinach

2 onions
3 tablespoons olive oil
1 lb. creamed cottage
    cheese
4 eggs
¼ cup whole wheat
    bread crumbs

Soak the feta cheese, in milk to cover, overnight. Wash spinach, remove tough stems and steam in little or no water for 3 minutes; just until beginning to wilt. Chop. Sauté onions in oil until transparent and slightly browned. Add spinach and cook for one minute. Beat together feta, cottage cheese and eggs. Stir in bread crumbs and spinach.

Place 3 layers of Phyllo pastry in large baking pan, brushing each sheet with melted margarine. Spoon on spinach mixture. Cover filling with 2–3 more layers of Phyllo, again brushing margarine between each. Tuck under dough to make edge and brush top with melted margarine. Bake at 350° F. for 40 minutes.

DEEP DISH SPINACH PIE

Filling:

2 pounds spinach (or beet tops), raw, washed, cut into bite-size pieces

½ cup parsley (chopped)

1 cup green onions (chopped)

⅛ teaspoon vegetable salt

½ teaspoon rosemary

2 tablespoons oil

Enough whole wheat pie crust dough for single crust

Place all ingredients in pan. Cook briefly, stirring once or twice, over low heat, only long enough to reduce ingredients to half their original bulk. Turn into oiled casserole. Cover with piecrust. Brush with cream. Bake at 425° F. for 15–20 minutes, only long enough to brown pastry.

STUFFED CABBAGE LEAVES

1 head cabbage (not a solid head)

1½ cups steamed brown rice

2 onions (sliced and steamed)

2 eggs

Parsley, thyme, sage

2 tablespoons whole wheat cracker or bread crumbs

3 cups tomato puree (see Soups chapter)

Steam cabbage briefly. Mix rice, steamed onions, eggs, minced parsley, seasonings and cracker crumbs. Remove cabbage leaves from water. When cool, place a tablespoon of the mixture in each cabbage leaf, roll up part way, then turn in the ends and continue rolling. Press between palms of hands gently. Place stuffed cabbage leaves in a casserole or roasting pan. Pour tomato puree over cabbage leaves. Bake in a slow oven (350°) for about 30 minutes.

CABBAGE WITH APPLES

1 head red cabbage (sliced)	¼ cup oil
2 cups apples (cut in chunks)	Cloves
3 tablespoons apple juice	Allspice
	1 cup yogurt

Simmer cabbage, apples, apple juice, oil and spices over low heat for 30 minutes, stirring when necessary. Add yogurt and cook about 5 minutes more.

SCALLOPED BRUSSELS SPROUTS

Remove wilted leaves from one pound of Brussels sprouts. Steam until tender. Wash and cut fine sufficient celery to make 1½ cups. Melt 3 tablespoons margarine. Add the celery. Steam two minutes. Add 3 tablespoons whole wheat flour. Pour in slowly 1½ cups scalded milk. Pour prepared mixture over sprouts. Cover with whole wheat bread crumbs. Dot with margarine. Bake in hot oven until crumbs are brown.

BEAN CAKE

Bean Cake is also known as Tofu or soy cheese. Bean cake is precipitated soy bean milk. It is very high in vegetable protein, can be used in soups and enjoyed in much the same way as cottage cheese. Bean Cake can be kept up to one week if submerged in a bowl of water, and kept in refrigerator.

1 cup full-fat soy flour	2 cups boiling water
1 cup cold water	Juice of 2 lemons

Beat soy flour into cold water with wire whisk, mixer or blender. Pour into boiling water and cook 5 minutes. Add lemon juice. Cool. Strain through cheesecloth and pack into square container.

BEAN CAKE AND ONIONS

1 lb. Bean Cake (Tofu) *	½ tablespoon corn starch
3 onions (sliced)	½ tablespoon soy sauce
4 tablespoons oil	
¾ cup water	

Sauté onions in oil until wilted. Drain bean cake and cut into one inch squares. Add bean cake to onions and stir. Mix corn starch, soy sauce and water. Pour over bean cakes. Simmer and stir until well heated and sauce is thickened.

* See instructions for making Bean Cakes, this chapter. Tofu can also be purchased in most Chinese and Japanese groceries.

EGG FOO YUNG

6–8 eggs	3 scallions (minced)
¼ cup water chestnuts (minced)	1 tablespoon honey
	1 cup bean sprouts
3 stalks celery with tops (minced)	¼ cup margarine

Beat eggs and stir in finely minced vegetables and honey. If a blender is used, this can be done quickly by breaking eggs into blender container, adding vegetables cut in pieces, and honey. Blend, using "medium" or "chop" blender speed for 10 seconds. Add bean sprouts but do not blend. Melt margarine in large skillet. Pour in ¼ cup egg-sprout mixture for each patty. Sauté over medium heat until brown. Turn and brown on other side. Keep patties warm in oven. Serve plain or with Chinese gravy.

Chinese Gravy:

2½ cups water
¼ cup soy sauce

2 tablespoons cornstarch or 1 tablespoon arrowroot

Blend well. Cook over low heat until clear.

PEA PODS AND BEAN SPROUTS

2 lbs. edible pea pods
1 lb. fresh bean sprouts
1 large onion (chopped)
½ green pepper (chopped)
1 stalk celery (chopped)

3 tablespoons oil
1 tablespoon soy sauce
1 tablespoon cornstarch or ½ tablespoon arrowroot
1 cup water

Clean pea pods, removing tips and strings. Cut in half if necessary. Sauté onion, pepper and celery in oil until wilted. Add pea pods and bean sprouts and ½ cup of water. Cover and steam until wilted about 7–8 minutes. Mix soy sauce, corn starch and remaining water together. Pour over vegetables and cook a few minutes longer to thicken sauce. Stir occasionally. A cup or so of cubed bean cake can be added to this dish.

CHINESE VEGETABLES

1 cup onions (sliced thin)
1 cup green peppers (chopped)
1 cup celery and tops (chopped)

½ cup mushrooms (sliced)
¼ cup oil
1 cup mung bean sprouts

Sauté onions, green peppers, celery and mushrooms briefly in oil. Remove from heat and stir in remaining ingredients.

111

STEAMED BEAN SPROUTS

1 onion (chopped)
1 tablespoon oil or
   margarine

¼ cup water
4 cups bean sprouts

Sauté onion briefly. Add water and sprouts. Steam just a very short time until sprouts begin to wilt. Add small dash of soy sauce, if desired.

PEAS WITH LEMON-MINT SAUCE

3 cups fresh, shelled
   peas
¼ cup margarine
1 tablespoon lemon
   juice

¼ teaspoon lemon peel
   (finely grated)
2 tablespoons fresh
   mint (finely
   chopped)

Steam peas in small amount of water for about 15 minutes. Stir in remaining ingredients. Serve immediately.

STEAMED BROCCOLI

Carefully wash broccoli. Tie in bunches and stand up in deep kettle, add water ¼ way up stalks, cover tightly and steam until tender.

BAKED CAULIFLOWER

Steam a large cauliflower. When tender, place in oiled casserole and alternate layers of cauliflower and whole wheat bread crumbs (toasted, if desired), each layer dotted with margarine. Continue until ingredients are used up. Make top layer of bread crumbs. Over this pour a cup of milk. Bake until brown. Seasoning may be used, if desired.

BAKED EGGPLANT WITH TOMATO

Bake one large eggplant about 20 minutes in a 400° oven until tender. Cut into slices about one inch thick. Place in a baking dish, alternating layers of sliced eggplant and slices of raw (or cooked) tomato. Season with chopped onion and green pepper, sprinkled over each layer of tomato. Dribble on tablespoonfuls of oil. Bake 20–30 minutes in a 400° oven. Serve from the baking dish.

EGGPLANT ROLLS

1 cup mozzarella
    cheese (grated)
½ cup Parmesan
    cheese (grated)
⅓ cup ricotta cheese
½ teaspoon oregano
2 eggs
1 tablespoon parsley
    (chopped)

2 tablespoons whole
    wheat flour
½ teaspoon baking
    powder
Vegetable salt to taste
⅓ cup milk
5 tablespoons olive oil
1 large eggplant

Combine cheese, one egg yolk (save the white), parsley and pinch of vegetable salt. Blend well. Beat the egg white stiffly and fold in. Place in refrigerator during next steps.

Make a batter out of the flour, baking powder, milk, remaining egg and one tablespoon of oil. Beat well. Peel the eggplant and cut in half the long way. Cut thin lengthwise slices (about $\frac{1}{16}$ inch). Flour slices lightly and dip into the batter. Brown slices in olive oil and drain on paper towels.

Place a dollop of cheese mixture on each slice and roll up. Then place rolls in an oiled baking dish and bake at 375° F. long enough to melt the cheese.

STRING BEANS IN HERB SAUCE

1 onion (sliced)
2 tablespoons oil
1 clove garlic (minced)
1 tablespoon celery
    (chopped)
1 tomato (cut in
    pieces)

1 tablespoon green
    pepper (minced)
¼ teaspoon savory
1 tablespoon parsley
1 whole clove
2 pounds string beans
    (lightly steamed)

Sauté onion in oil. Add remaining ingredients, except string beans. Cover. Simmer gently for 10 minutes. Pour over beans.

OLIVE-STUFFED PEPPERS

5–6 bell peppers
1 cup of ripe olives
    (seeded and
    chopped)
2 cups whole wheat
    bread crumbs

1 cup grated cheese
1 cup milk
1 egg
1 small onion (chopped
    fine)

Cut off tops of medium-sized bell peppers and remove seeds. Mix all ingredients. Fill peppers with the mixture. Place a small piece of margarine on the top of each pepper. Bake slowly in an oiled baking dish for 45 minutes in a 350° oven.

RICE-STUFFED PEPPERS

6 large bell peppers
1 cup steamed brown
    rice
1 minced raw onion
4 tablespoons olive oil

2 tablespoons chopped
    parsley
1 clove garlic (minced)
Sage
Thyme
2 cups tomato purée

Sauté onion, parsley and garlic in oil. Mix rice, herbs and sautéed vegetables together. Cut off tops of peppers; clean out seeds and fill with the rice mixture. Place in casserole. Blend one tablespoon of olive oil into tomato purée. Pour purée over ingredients. Bake at 350° F. until done (approx. 30–40 minutes).

SOYBEANS

4 cups sprouted
  soybeans
3 tablespoons soy oil
1 green pepper
  (chopped)

½ cup onion
  (chopped)
¼ cup olives
  (chopped)

Sauce:
2 cups tomatoes
2 tablespoons honey

Vegetable salt to taste

Soybeans are cooked for 20 minutes. Onion and green pepper with chopped olives are lightly browned in oil and cooked 20 minutes. Beans and sauce are combined and heated before serving.

VEGETABLE-SOYBEAN LOAF

1 cup raw carrots
  (grated)
1 cup soybeans
  (cooked)
1 cup raw beets
  (grated)
1 onion (grated)
1 green pepper
  (minced)

3 tablespoons soy flour
½ cup wheat germ
⅓ cup tomato juice
2 eggs
½ teaspoon vegetable
  salt
1 teaspoon oregano
1 teaspoon parsley

Blend all ingredients. Turn into oiled loaf pan. Bake at 350° F. for about 1 hour.

CELERIAC CASSEROLE

1 lb. celeriac (thinly   3 tablespoons
   sliced)   margarine
¼ lb. cheese   1 cup hot milk
   (shredded)   Vegetable salt to taste

Place alternate layers of celeriac slices and
cheese in oiled baking dish. Pour over the hot
milk, dot with margarine and bake at 350° F.
for 30–40 minutes.

BAKED ASPARAGUS

2 lbs. steamed   1 tablespoon
   asparagus   margarine
1 cup bread crumbs   Seasoning to taste

Cut the asparagus into inch lengths. Place in
layers in an oiled baking dish. Sprinkle bread
crumbs, celery salt and paprika between each
layer. Over all pour juice left after steaming
asparagus. Bake 20 minutes in 300° oven. Just
before removing from oven, sprinkle top thickly
with grated cheese. Let melt. Serve.

STEAMED ASPARAGUS

Cut off lower part of stalks as far down as
they will snap. Place stalks of asparagus (about
2 lbs.) together and stand in deep covered
kettle with water ¼ way up stalks. Steam until
tender (5 minutes or less). Serve with one of the
following: margarine, yogurt, lemon juice,
cheese sauce. Season with celery salt, tarragon
or vegetable salt.

ASPARAGUS ON TOAST WITH MUSHROOM SAUCE

2–3 lbs. asparagus tips
½ pound mushrooms
4 teaspoons margarine
1 teaspoon celery salt

4 tablespoons whole wheat flour
2 cups milk
6 slices whole wheat toast

Steam asparagus. Wash mushrooms thoroughly. Chop up or slice mushrooms. Make a sauce by melting margarine and adding flour and seasonings. Pour in the milk slowly, stirring constantly until smooth. Add the mushrooms and cook until they are tender. When ready to serve, place asparagus tips on toast and pour sauce over them.

BROILED TOMATOES

6 large tomatoes (unpeeled)
1 cup whole wheat bread crumbs
2 tablespoons green onions (chopped)
¼ teaspoon oregano

¼ teaspoon basil
¼ teaspoon vegetable salt
2 tablespoons olive oil
½ cup Parmesan cheese

Mix together crumbs, chopped onions, herbs and salt. Dip ¾ inch slices of tomato into crumb mixture. Pour oil in shallow pan and put in well-coated slices. Place under broiler for about 2 minutes. Remove, sprinkle with Parmesan cheese and broil just long enough to melt cheese.

TOMATOES AND OKRA

¼ cup onion
  (chopped)
1 small garlic clove
  (minced)
2 cups sliced okra
2 tablespoons oil or
  margarine

2 cups cooked
  tomatoes
¼ teaspoon oregano
½ teaspoon vegetable
  salt
Parsley

Brown onion, garlic and okra in oil. Add tomatoes and seasonings. Cook over moderate heat
until okra is tender and mixture thickens. Add a
little chopped parsley before serving.

BAKED TOMATOES

Several firm, large
  tomatoes
Olive oil
Lemon juice

Tarragon
Parsley
Ground coriander
  seeds

Wash tomatoes. Make small hole in the top of
each tomato and put a little vegetable salt into
each one. Rub tomatoes with olive oil and put
them carefully, cut-side down, into a shallow
baking pan. Add a small amount of water and
lemon juice to the bottom of pan. Sprinkle with
parsley and coriander. Bake for 10 minutes at
300°F. Baste occasionally with pan liquid.

STUFFED TOMATOES

6 large tomatoes

Stuffing:
1 cup rice (cooked)
2 mushrooms
  (chopped)
1 onion (chopped)
1 tablespoon oil
½ teaspoon thyme

½ teaspoon vegetable
  salt
½ cup celery and tops
  (diced and
  steamed)

Fill cavities with stuffing. Put tomatoes in oiled baking pan. Bake at 350°F. for 30–35 minutes.

BAKED BEANS AND TOMATOES

1 qt. navy beans
3 cups tomatoes
(chopped)

2 tablespoons honey
Vegetable salt to taste

Soak beans overnight. Simmer beans in own liquid for one hour. Combine with remaining ingredients and put into stoneware crock. Cover and bake in 250° oven 3–4 hours or until tender. Remove cover and allow to brown. Serve.

BAKED ONIONS

6 onions (preferably Bermuda)
4 slices toast (rye or whole wheat)
1 cup milk

3 tablespoons margarine
4 eggs
1 cup cheddar cheese (grated)

Cut onions in ½-inch slices and steam for 4–5 minutes. Cut toast in half, butter and place in the bottom of a casserole. Place onions on top of toast and cover with grated cheese. Mix beaten eggs and milk together and pour over all. Place dabs of margarine on the top and bake for 30 minutes at 350° F.

VEGETABLE STEW

2 onions (sliced)
2 tablespoons oil
1 cup raw potato (cubed)
1 cup zucchini (sliced)
1 cup yellow squash (sliced)
½ cup carrot (grated)

½ cup parsnip (grated)
3 tomatoes (cut in wedges)
3 tablespoons brewers' yeast
3 tablespoons parsley (minced)
1 sprig dill (minced)

Sauté onions until clear. Add all other ingredients. Simmer until tender with cover on.

SUMMER SQUASH

Slice the squash the round way. Dip the slices in beaten egg and then in whole wheat or cracker crumbs. Place on an oiled pan and bake underneath the broiler flame until brown and tender, turning once.

YELLOW CROOK-NECK SQUASH

½ onion (chopped)   **Vegetable salt to taste**
7 crook-neck squash   **Dash of fresh nutmeg**
3 tablespoons olive oil
    or margarine

Slice squash about ½ inch thick into oiled frying pan. Add chopped onions, salt, nutmeg and 2 or 3 tablespoons of water. Cook until squash are tender.

BAKED GRATED ZUCCHINI

6–7 medium zucchini   ¼ cup margarine
Parmesan cheese

Grate zucchini into oiled casserole, approximately 13 x 8 x 2. Dab top with margarine and sprinkle with Parmesan cheese. Place in preheated 400° oven for 10 or 15 minutes until margarine is melted. Do not overcook; zucchini should be a little crunchy.

STUFFED ZUCCHINI

2 or 3 large zucchini   ⅛ teaspoon rosemary
¾ cup whole wheat   ⅛ teaspoon marjoram
    bread crumbs   ¼ teaspoon oregano
2 tablespoons   ¼ teaspoon sage
    Parmesan cheese

Scoop out centers of partly-steamed zucchini to make ¾ cup. Take this pulp and add to it the above ingredients. Stuff zucchini shells with the mixture. Bake 10 minutes in 350°F. oven. Sprinkle with Parmesan cheese.

ZUCCHINI PANCAKES

4–5 medium zucchini
3 eggs, whole
4 tablespoons whole
   wheat flour
3 tablespoons
   Parmesan cheese
   (grated)
1 teaspoon parsley
Pinch of garlic powder

Grate zucchini, stir in rest of ingredients. Oil skillet or pancake griddle and heat to usual pancake temperature. Drop batter onto skillet and cook until brown. Turn over and brown on other side. Place on platter in warm oven. Serve with dab of margarine.

SAUCY CUCUMBERS

4 cucumbers (sliced)
2 tablespoons oil
2 tablespoons onions
   (sliced)
¼ cup yogurt
2 tablespoons honey
4 tablespoons lemon
   juice

Sauté onions in oil until transparent. Mix yogurt, honey and lemon juice and blend with cucumbers and cooled onions.

BAKED SQUASH

3 small squash (acorn,
   butternut, etc.)
3 tablespoons honey
3 tablespoons oil or
   margarine
⅛ teaspoon mace
   (ground)
½ cup sesame seeds

Cut squash in half. Remove seeds and membranes. Arrange in shallow pan. Fill pan ¼ inch high with water. Blend remaining ingredients together. Spoon mixture into cavity of squash. Cover and bake at 350° F. for about 1 hour, uncovering during the last 10 minutes of baking time to allow to brown.

GRATED TURNIPS

5–6 medium turnips Vegetable salt to taste
3 tablespoons
 margarine

Wash and grate unpeeled turnips. Place in oiled baking dish, dot top with margarine, and slip into preheated 400° F. oven for 6–10 minutes. Turnips should be served while still crunchy.

PARSNIPS IN CIDER

8 parsnips ⅓ cup brown sugar
6 tablespoons ⅔ cup cider
 margarine

Peel, core and cut parsnips in quarters, lengthwise. Cook in water to cover until almost tender. Place in baking dish. Mix rest of ingredients and spread over parsnips. Bake for 20 minutes at 400° F. Baste occasionally.

BAKED BEETS

Scrub 1 bunch of beets well. Place in baking dish with ½–1 cup of water and 1 tablespoon of olive oil. Cover dish and bake at 350° F. for 1–1½ hours depending upon size of the beets. Serve whole or cubed.

BEETS AND TOPS

4 beets with tops
Vegetable salt to taste
1 tablespoon
    margarine

2 tablespoons lemon
    juice

Wash beets and tops well. Cut away tops and steam in their own moisture until wilted. Grate beets and add to tops, along with margarine and vegetable salt. Simmer for about 5 minutes. Stir in lemon juice. Serve.

SWEET POTATOES BAKED WITH HONEY

6 sweet potatoes or
    yams, cooked and
    cut in half
    lengthwise

½ cup honey
Juice of 1 lemon
¼ cup oil
Pinch of mace

Arrange sweet potatoes in oiled casserole. Mix remaining ingredients together. Pour mixture over potatoes. Bake at 350° F. for about 30 minutes, basting occasionally with liquid.

BAKED POTATO CASSEROLE

Slice raw potatoes. Place a layer in a baking dish. Dot with margarine. Sprinkle well with minced onion and minced parsley. Add another layer of sliced potatoes. Sprinkle with minced onion and parsley. Dot with margarine. Continue this until the dish is filled. Add enough water to cover bottom of pan. Dot top with margarine. Cover. Let bake slowly in 375° oven about 45 minutes or until potatoes are tender. Remove cover and brown.

POTATOES AU GRATIN

In a baking dish place a layer of potatoes that have been steamed and diced. Over this sprinkle thickly grated cheese. Dot with margarine. Repeat until baking dish is almost filled. Place a layer of whole wheat bread crumbs dotted with margarine over the top. Pour milk over to just cover. Bake for 30 minutes in a 375° oven. Let brown. (New potatoes are especially good in this recipe.)

STUFFED POTATOES

Bake even-sized potatoes 45 minutes to 1 hour in 425° oven. Cut in half lengthwise. Scoop out inside. Mash with margarine, finely minced onion and yogurt. Beat very well. Replace in shells. Brown in oven. Just before serving, sprinkle with minced parsley, and add a dot of margarine.

POTATO PANCAKES

5 scrubbed potatoes	1 onion (grated)
1 egg	Vegetable salt to taste
¼ cup parsley (chopped)	Oil or margarine

Grate potatoes finely. Add the rest of ingredients and mix well. Heat heavy skillet and add oil, then drop batter from a large spoon onto skillet. Brown on one side, then turn and cook until golden brown on other side.

BAKED POTATOES IN JACKETS

Select potatoes of uniform size. Scrub well and dry. Brush with vegetable oil. The skins will then be tender and edible. Cut off tip ends. Bake in a moderately hot oven (425°) about 50 minutes or until tender. Serve with margarine. (Remember that the skins contain important nutrients and should be eaten whenever possible.)

NUT LOAF

1½ cups nut meats (chopped)
3 cups whole wheat bread crumbs
1 cup celery (finely chopped)

½ cup onion (finely chopped)
2 eggs
3 tablespoons oil
1 cup tomato juice
¼ cup parsley
Vegetable salt to taste

Mix all ingredients together. Pack into oiled loaf pan and bake at 350° F. for about 45 minutes.

MACARONI AND CHEESE

2 cups vegetable macaroni noodles or shell macaroni
2 cups water
1½ cups raw milk

½ cup powdered non-fat milk
1 cup grated cheddar cheese

Bring water to boil and slowly add macaroni. Cover and simmer until almost tender. Remove from heat, drain and add the milk, milk powder and cheese. Mix well. Pour into oiled baking dish. If desired, make crumb topping by mixing ⅔ cup whole wheat bread crumbs with 4 tablespoons margarine, and sprinkle on top. Brown at 300° F. for 15 minutes.

CHEESE SOUFFLE

4 tablespoons margarine
4 tablespoons whole wheat flour
1 cup milk

½ teaspoon thyme
1½ cup cheddar cheese (grated)
6 eggs (separated)

Melt margarine, stir in flour. Add milk and cheese slowly, stirring constantly over low heat. Add thyme and cook until smooth and thick. Remove from heat and blend in 6 well-beaten egg yolks and dash of vegetable salt. Fold in stiffly beaten whites of 6 eggs. Pour into oiled souffle dish or baking dish with straight sides about ¾ inch high. Bake uncovered at 350° F. for 1 hour until golden brown and top puffs up high.

TOAST WITH CHEESE SAUCE

2 cups certified milk
2 eggs
2 tablespoons
    margarine

1 lb. sharp cheddar
    cheese
4 slices rye or whole
    wheat bread

Toast bread and spread with margarine. Place on warm plates. Beat eggs and add milk, margarine and cheese. Heat and stir until smooth in double-boiler. Pour over toast.

BLENDER SPINACH SOUFFLE

1 lb. spinach
    (steamed)
1 cup stock or water
3 tablespoons
    whole wheat flour

¼ teaspoon vegetable
    salt
3 tablespoons brewers'
    yeast
¼ cup cheese (grated)
4 eggs (separated)

Put all ingredients except egg whites in blender and blend until smooth. Fold in stiffly-beaten egg whites. Turn into oiled casserole or oiled individual custard cups. Bake at 375° F. for 35–40 minutes.

BREADS

BANANA BREAD

4 tablespoons oil or ½
   cup margarine
½ cup honey, or ⅔
   cup raw sugar
3 eggs (beaten)
3–4 ripe bananas
   (mashed)
2 cups whole wheat
   pastry flour

3 teaspoons baking
   powder
¼ teaspoon salt
⅓ cup pecans or
   raisins (chopped)
⅔ cup milk
½ teaspoon vanilla

Cream oil and sugar together. Add eggs and bananas and beat. Sift dry ingredients together and add to banana mixture. Add nuts or raisins, milk and vanilla. Beat well. Pour batter into oiled loaf pan and bake at 350° F. for 50 minutes.

SOYA-RICE FLOUR RAISIN BREAD

¼ cup raw milk
2 eggs (beaten)
½ cup honey or raw
   sugar
¼ cup safflower oil
½ cup soya flour

1½ cups brown rice
   flour
1 teaspoon baking
   powder
½ cup raisins
¼ cup nuts (chopped)

Mix milk, eggs, honey, and oil. Sift dry ingredients and add slowly. Stir in raisins and nuts. Pour into oiled bread pan. Let stand for 1 hour. Bake in moderate oven (350° F.) about 45 minutes.

WHEAT GERM MUFFINS

1 cup milk
1 egg (beaten)
3 tablespoons honey
3 tablespoons oil
1 cup wheat germ

1 cup whole wheat
   flour
½ teaspoon salt
4 teaspoons baking
   powder

Mix milk, egg, honey and oil together. Add wheat germ and mix well. Sift together flour, salt and baking powder. Add to wheat germ mixture. Mix well. Oil muffin pan or line with pleated paper muffin cups. Fill half-way with batter and bake in pre-heated oven at 400° F. for 20 minutes.

WHOLE WHEAT MUFFINS

2 cups sifted whole
   wheat flour
¼ teaspoon salt
3 teaspoons baking
   powder

3 tablespoons oil
1 egg (beaten)
1 cup milk
¼ cup honey
½ cup seedless raisins

Sift flour, salt and baking powder together. Blend oil, egg, milk, and honey. Stir into flour mixture. Add raisins. Do not beat. Batter should be lumpy. Pour into oiled muffin tin. Bake in preheated 375° F. oven for 20 minutes.

CORNBREAD

2 cups corn meal
½ teaspoon salt
2 teaspoons baking
powder

2 tablespoons oil
1 cup milk
1 egg (beaten)
1 tablespoon raw
sugar

Sift together corn meal, salt and baking powder. Add oil, milk, egg and sugar. Mix well. Pour into oiled 8-inch square pan. Bake in preheated oven at 400° F. for 30 minutes.

SUNFLOWER OAT BREAD

2 cups rolled oats
2 cups boiling water
½ teaspoon salt
2 tablespoons active
dry yeast
¼ cup lukewarm
water
1 tablespoon oil

¾ cup hulled
sunflower seeds
½ cup gluten flour*
½ cup soya flour
4 cups unbleached
white or whole
wheat flour

Pour boiling water over the oats and let stand for 1 hour. Add yeast, dissolved in lukewarm water, to oat mixture. Mix in remaining ingredients. Knead until smooth and elastic, adding more flour if needed. Cover and let rise in warm place until double in bulk. Knead down again, shape into loaves and place in loaf pans greased with margarine. Cover and let rise until higher than sides of pan. Bake at 350° F. for about 1 hour.

* Gluten is a wheat protein that increases the volume of yeast breads.

SPROUTED WHEAT BREAD

Wheat sprouts (finely
    chopped)

(3 days in advance, prepare sprouts by following instructions on sprouting and using ten
tablespoons whole wheat grain.)

3 cups lukewarm   1 tablespoon salt
    (110° F.) water   ¼ cup honey
2 tablespoons dry   3 tablespoons oil or
    active yeast   melted margarine
5½ cups stone-ground whole wheat flour or
    unbleached white, or a combination of both

Dissolve yeast in 1 cup lukewarm water in very
large warm bowl. Add honey, salt, oil and the
rest of the water. Stir in, a little at a time, 3½
cups flour. Beat dough well until elastic. This
step is important in developing the gluten which
gives good texture and volume to the loaf.

Let rise in warm (85° F.) place. When doubled
in size, punch down and knead in chopped
sprouts and 2 cups of flour. Place in oiled bowl.
Turn over once to oil top. Cover with clean towel
and let rise once more until double in size.
Knead lightly. Shape into loaves. Place in loaf
pans that have been greased with margarine.
Let rise until higher than sides of pan. Bake at
350° F. for 45 minutes. Brush top with melted
margarine when done. Turn out on wire rack to
cool.

GRAINS

SWISS BREAKFAST
(Uncooked)

6 apples (grated)
3 tablespoons honey
1 cup fresh berries (if available)
Juice of 2 lemons

¼ cup ground nuts (hazelnuts, almonds)
½ cup yogurt
½ cup raw oats, soaked overnight in one cup water

Mix all ingredients together. Serve with orange juice, milk, or top with dollop of yogurt and a fresh berry or two.

GOOD MORNING!
(Uncooked)

½ cup raisins
½ cup hulled
    sunflower seeds
Juice of one lemon
1 cup water

½ cup wheat germ
3 bananas (sliced)
2 apples (grated)
1 cup yogurt

Soak raisins and sunflower seeds in water and lemon for 1 hour. Mix in wheat germ, apples and bananas, and top with yogurt.

ENZYME VITAMIN CEREAL
(Uncooked)

7 tablespoons wheat
    germ
3 teaspoons chia seeds
2 teaspoons sunflower
    seed meal
4 teaspoons brewers'
    yeast

3 teaspoons sesame
    seeds
2 tablespoons raw
    sugar
3 teaspoons rice polish

Mix together and serve with milk, fruit or orange juice.

WHEAT CEREAL
(Uncooked)

½ cup raisins
2 cups cracked wheat

4 cups water

Mix together and soak overnight.

THERMOS BOTTLE COOKED CEREAL

⅔ cup whole wheat
    grain
⅓ cup whole oats

1 tablespoon hulled
    sunflower seeds
⅓ cup hulled barley
4 cups water

Mix ingredients and soak all day. That evening,

drain and save water. Add sufficient water to saved water to total 3 cups in all. Boil water, add grain and boil 1 minute. Pour into 1 qt. thermos bottle and turn on side overnight.

STEAMED BROWN RICE

1 cup brown rice (raw) 2 cups water

Boil water and sprinkle in rice. Cover and cook gently for 30–40 minutes, until all liquid is absorbed. Serve with milk or yogurt and fruit. Honey may be used to sweeten.

STEAMED BUCKWHEAT GROATS

1 cup buckwheat groats   **¼ teaspoon salt (if desired)**
2 cups water

Sprinkle buckwheat slowly into boiling water. Stir for 1 minute. Reduce heat to gentle simmer, cover pot, and cook 15 minutes. Can be served with honey, milk or yogurt and fruit. May also be served in place of rice or potatoes with a little margarine, if desired.

DESSERTS

BLENDER APPLESAUCE
(Raw)

3–4 crisp apples
    (Jonathans or
    Gravensteins)
1 tablespoon lemon
    juice

¼ cup honey
¼ to ½ cup apple
    cider

Wash, core and slice apples. Peel if they have been sprayed, otherwise leave unpeeled. Place cider, honey and lemon juice in blender container and add apples until ⅓ full. Using "blend," or "medium-fast speed," blend and add the rest of the apple slices until all have been used. Chill and serve.

CRISPY TOPPED APPLES

6–8 apples (preferably Pippin)
¼ teaspoon nutmeg
¼ teaspoon cinnamon
½ cup apple cider
½ cup raisins

Topping:
½ cup whole wheat flour (pastry)
1 cup brown sugar
¼ cup sesame seeds
3 tablespoons margarine

Wash, core and slice apples. Peel if sprayed, otherwise leave unpeeled. Mix with raisins, place in oiled casserole. Sprinkle on spices and pour cider over apples. Work topping ingredients with fingers until crumbly. Spread over apples and bake uncovered at 375° F. until apples are tender.

STEWED APPLES

1½ lbs. firm, unsprayed apples
¾ cup water
3 tablespoons raw sugar or honey
1 tablespoon lemon juice

Core unpeeled apples and cut in one-half inch slices. (If unsprayed apples are not available, peel them.) Simmer slices in water until barely tender. Add sugar and lemon. Simmer 1 minute more. Let cool and serve with liquid.

BAKED APPLES

4 or more large apples (Rome Beauty)
½ cup raw sugar
Cinnamon, nutmeg, clove, to taste

Peel upper ¼ of cored apples and place peeled side down into ½ cup boiling water in large pan. Simmer until tender (about 10 minutes). Turn apples, peeled side up, and sprinkle with spices and sugar. Brown in 450° oven.

STEWED PEARS

3 pears
1 cup orange juice,
   fresh or frozen

¼ cup honey or 2
   tablespoons raw
   sugar
1 teaspoon orange rind
   (grated)

Wash pears, core and cut in half. Simmer in orange juice until tender. Lift out pears and add sweetener and orange rind to juice. Simmer syrup 3 minutes longer. Pour over pears and chill.

BAKED PEARS

6 pears (unpeeled)
¼ cup honey
¼ cup lemon juice

2 tablespoons oil or
   melted margarine

Cut pears in half and place in oiled baking dish, cut side up. Blend honey, lemon juice and oil together and pour over pears. Bake at 350° F. for about 15 minutes. Serve hot or cold.

FRUIT DESSERT SUPREME

1 cup bananas (sliced)
1 cup oranges (sliced)
1 cup pineapple
   (sliced)
1 cup pears (sliced)

½ cup nuts (pecans or
   walnuts)
1 egg yolk (beaten)
1 cup yogurt
1 tablespoon honey
Nutmeg to taste

Mix fruits together. Pour over the remaining combined ingredients and chill at least 1 hour before serving.

COOKED DRIED FRUIT COMPOTE

Wash dried fruit of your choice. Place in pan with tight fitting lid. Add small amount of water and steam over low fire about 45 minutes. Add more water if needed. This water makes an excellent beverage, cold or heated.

UNCOOKED DRIED FRUIT COMPOTE

Soak washed, dried fruits of your choice in apple cider or orange juice overnight. Yogurt makes an excellent topping, if desired.

FRUIT CUP

6–8 apricots
1–2 oranges (diced)
1 banana (sliced)

½ cup fresh or frozen
berries

Cut apricots into small sections. Mix together gently with other fruit. Sweeten to taste with honey, and chill.

FIG AMBROSIA

1 lb. fresh figs
3 large oranges
5 tablespoons coconut
(grated)

8 tablespoons orange
juice
½ teaspoon orange
peel (grated)
2 tablespoons honey

Wash and slice figs. Peel oranges, separate segments, remove membranes and seeds. Toss all ingredients together and chill.

FRUIT JUICE GELATIN

½ cup vegetable
gelatin
(agar-agar)
1½ cups water

2 cups fruit juice of
your choice
¼ cup honey

Dissolve agar-agar in water for a few minutes. Simmer a few more minutes until dissolved.

Add fruit juice, sweeten with honey if needed, and allow to set. It will jell rapidly.

BLUEBERRIES IN YOGURT

2 cups blueberries   3 tablespoons honey
   (fresh if possible;   1 cup yogurt
   otherwise, frozen)

Mix together and chill. If desired, strawberries or peaches may be used in place of blueberries.

BERRY YOGURT

1 cup plain yogurt   ¼ cup honey
3 cups strawberries,
   blueberries or
   raspberries

Blend ¼ cup of berries together with other ingredients in blender; spoon over the remaining berries. Chill and serve.

BAKED QUINCE

3 or 4 quinces   Fresh ginger root
10 tablespoons brown   (thinly sliced)
   sugar

Wash, core and peel quinces. Cut in quarters. Place in oiled casserole and add ½ inch water. Sprinkle sugar over quinces and add ginger. Bake, covered, at 300° F. for 2 hours, until tender.

BAKED RHUBARB

1½ lbs. rhubarb   1 cup fresh berries
1½ cups raisins   Mace
⅓ cup pineapple,
   orange or apple
   juice

Cut rhubarb into chunks. Leach out oxalic acid by pouring boiling water over rhubarb. Let stand 10 minutes, then pour off liquid. Mix rhubarb with raisins and fruit juice and place in oiled casserole. Cover and bake at 350° F. for about 25 minutes. Serve with garnish of fresh berries. Sprinkle with mace.

BROILED BANANAS

Slice bananas lengthwise, dot with bits of margarine and sprinkle with raw sugar and mace. Broil until lightly browned.

PRUNE WHIP

2 cups prunes
¼ cup pignolias or
    almonds

Honey to taste

Soak prunes overnight in spring water or apple juice. Remove pits and blend with the soaking liquid in blender. Add nuts and mix well. Add honey if needed.

BANANA LEMON SAUCE

2 ripe bananas
Juice of one lemon
Rind of ½ lemon
Handful of raisins

3–4 ozs. cream cheese
    (cut in cubes)
½ cup honey
½ cup raw sugar

Put all ingredients in blender container and blend until smooth. Serve over plain cake or pudding.

RAW CRANBERRY SAUCE

1 cup fresh
    cranberries
½ ripe banana
Juice of 1 orange

1 tablespoon orange
    rind (grated)
1 apple

Place above ingredients in blender container and blend at "whip," or "medium" speed. Add honey if desired.

POLYNESIAN COCONUT PUDDING

5 tablespoons honey
3 tablespoons
  cornstarch or
  arrowroot

2 cups coconut milk
  (see Drinks)

Combine honey and cornstarch. Stir coconut milk into honey mixture slowly, stirring constantly, and heat until thickened. Do not boil. Pour into individual dishes and chill. One-half cup grated coconut can be added before coconut milk is stirred in. Top with sliced strawberries.

UNCOOKED HOLIDAY PUDDING

1 cup raisins and/or
  currants (minced)
2 pieces candied
  ginger (minced)
2 crisp apples (grated)
2 carrots (grated)
2 teaspoons orange
  rind (grated)

4 tablespoons orange
  juice
2 tablespoons candied
  orange peel
2 cups almonds
  (ground)
4 ozs. bread crumbs
¼ cup glacé cherries
Dash of mace

Mix together all ingredients. Press into oiled pudding mold or large bowl and put a weight on top. Age a few days in refrigerator or at least overnight.

DATE RICE PUDDING

1 qt. milk
½ cup raw sugar or
  honey
¼ cup uncooked brown
  rice

¼ teaspoon salt
¼ teaspoon nutmeg
1 cup dates (chopped)

Mix all ingredients, except dates, and pour into 2-quart casserole, greased with margarine. Bake at 300° F. for 1 hour. Stir occasionally to keep rice from settling. Then stir in dates and bake 2 hours more.

CARRAGEEN MOSS PUDDING

⅓ cup carrageen *
   (Irish moss)
3 cups milk (scalded)

4 tablespoons honey
   (or more, to taste)
1 egg (separated)
¼ teaspoon vanilla

Soak carrageen 10 minutes in water to cover, then drain. Mix with milk in saucepan. Simmer for 20 minutes. Strain, rubbing carrageen through sieve. Add honey, egg yolk and vanilla, and beat well. Beat egg white until stiff and fold into mixture. Chill and serve.

* Carrageen is seaweed. Seaweed is a natural tonic, rich in minerals and trace elements.

COTTAGE CHEESE CUSTARD

2 cups cottage cheese
2 eggs
¼ cup honey

2 tablespoons raisins
Cinnamon to taste

Mix all ingredients. Place in 1½ qt. casserole or baking dish. Bake in 325° oven for 20–25 minutes or until set.

RICE CUSTARD

⅓ cup brown rice
   (cooked)
2 cups milk

2 eggs
⅓ cup honey
1½ teaspoons vanilla
½ cup raisins

Combine and mix all ingredients. Pour into oiled

custard cups or baking dish and bake at 325° F. for about 1 hour, or until knife inserted in center comes out clean.

APRICOT CUSTARD

2 cups milk
½ cup non-sulphured
    dried apricots
⅓ cup honey
3 eggs

Place in blender container and blend at highest speed, making sure all unblended material is scraped off the sides of the container. Blend for about 3 minutes. Pour into oiled custard cups, place in pan of hot water and bake at 350° F. about 45 minutes until knife inserted into center comes out clean.

HONEY CARROT ICE CREAM

1 cup raw milk
1 cup raw cream
¾ cup honey
3 cups fresh carrot
    juice
2 teaspoons vanilla

Mix ingredients well and freeze in ice cream freezer. If unavailable, ice cream can be frozen in refrigerator freezer compartment as follows: Pour into shallow container and freeze until ice crystals have formed ¾ inch deep around container. Remove and beat well. Return to freezer until mushy but not quite solid. Remove and beat again. Replace in freezer until firm.

BANANA ORANGE SHERBERT

3 ripe bananas
1 cup orange juice
2 cups yogurt

Mash bananas and beat in remaining ingredients. Freeze in freezer compartment of refrigerator, beating once or twice during freezing process as described in previous recipe.

CAKES & PIES

WHOLE WHEAT PIE CRUST

1½ cups whole wheat   ½ cup wheat germ
    pastry flour   ⅔ cup margarine
½ teaspoon salt   ¼ cup ice water *

Sift flour and salt into large mixing bowl. Add
wheat germ. Cut margarine into flour with
pastry blender. (Mixture should look like pea-
sized crumbles.) Sprinkle in water and mix with
fork. (Handling and excessive mixing toughens
the crust.) Roll out on floured board a 10½
inch circle. Roll gently around rolling pin, and
unroll over 9 inch pie pan, depositing it inside,
with about ¾ inch overlapping. Tuck overlap
under and flute edge. If shell is baked first without filling, prick bottom with fork. Bake in
425° F. preheated oven for 8–10 minutes. Makes
2 single pie shells or 1 double crust.

    If double crust is desired, filling is put into

unbaked shell. Top crust is rolled out just as the bottom was, placed on top of the filling and overlap is tucked under. Flute edge and cut slits in crust for steam and excess juice to escape.

* Refrigerate small amount of bottled spring water until iced.

CRUMB CRUST

16 graham crackers *
3 tablespoons raw
   sugar
¼ teaspoon cinnamon
⅓ cup soft margarine

Roll graham crackers with rolling pin to make fine crumbs. Mix crumbs with rest of ingredients. Put in 9-inch pie pan and press firmly onto sides and bottom. Bake at 400° F. for 6 minutes.

* Stone-ground graham crackers are available in health food stores.

COCONUT PIE CRUST

1 cup coconut
   (shredded)
½ cup wheat germ
¼ cup whole wheat
   flour
2 tablespoons honey
2 tablespoons soft
   margarine

Mix all ingredients. Press into pie pan. Bake 5–7 minutes in preheated 400° F. oven.

PUMPKIN PIE

1 ¾ cups cooked
   pumpkin, or
   squash (mashed)
⅔ cup raw sugar
¼ teaspoon mace
1 teaspoon cinnamon
¼ teaspoon cloves
¼ teaspoon ginger
1 teaspoon salt
3 eggs (beaten)
2 cups milk
1 teaspoon vanilla

Mix all ingredients together. Pour into 9-inch unbaked pie shell. Bake at 450° F. 10 minutes, then lower heat to 325° F. and bake until silver knife inserted into center of pie comes out clean.

RAISIN SOUR CREAM PIE

2 eggs
⅞ cup raw sugar
1 cup sour cream

1 cup raisins
    (chopped)
1 teaspoon cinnamon

Beat all ingredients together. Pour into unbaked 9-inch pie shell. Bake at 450° F. for 10 minutes, then lower heat to 350° F. and bake 30 minutes longer.

LEMON CHEESE PIE

3 small packages
    cream cheese
1 tablespoon soft
    margarine
1 cup raw sugar
1 egg

2 tablespoons flour
⅔ cup milk
¼ cup lemon juice
2 tablespoons lemon
    rind (grated)

Cream margarine and sugar together, then add cream cheese and egg, and mix well. Add milk, lemon juice and rind, and beat. Pour into unbaked crumb or coconut crust. Bake at 350° F. for 35 minutes. Chill before serving.

CHEESE CAKE

Crust:
1 cup zwieback or
    graham cracker
    crumbs

¼ teaspoon cinnamon
3 tablespoons melted
    margarine

Cake:
3 8–oz. packages
    cream cheese
    (room
    temperature)

¼ teaspoon salt
1 teaspoon vanilla
4 egg whites
1 cup raw sugar

Topping:
1 pint sour cream
2 tablespoons raw
    sugar

⅛ teaspoon salt

Mix together the crust ingredients and press onto bottom of 9-inch spring-form pan.

Cream together cream cheese, salt and vanilla. Beat egg whites until stiff, then beat in sugar. Fold egg white mixture into cheese mixture. Turn into prepared pan and bake at 350° F. for 25 minutes.

Combine topping ingredients and spread on top of cake. Place in oven 5–7 minutes more until set. Cool, then chill.

This is probably the "richest" recipe in the book. Sour cream and a considerable amount of cream cheese are used. It is best saved for special occasions. If you're watching your weight closely, skip it.

CAROB CAKE

½ cup soft margarine
1⅔ cups raw sugar
2 eggs
½ cup carob powder
½ cup water

2½ cups whole wheat
   pastry flour
   (sifted)
½ teaspoon soda
½ teaspoon salt
⅓ cup yogurt
⅓ cup milk

Cream margarine and sugar, add eggs and beat. Mix water and carob powder and stir into sugar mixture. Sift dry ingredients together 2 times. Add ½ of dry ingredients to sugar, carob mixture, then add yogurt and milk combined. Mix well and add remainder of dry ingredients. Grease a large oblong cake pan, approximately 9 x 14 inches, with margarine. Pour in batter and bake at 350° F. for 30–35 minutes. When cool, cut in slices and serve with Banana Lemon Sauce (see Desserts chapter).

CANADIAN DATE CAKE

Filling:

1½ cups dates (chopped)

2 tablespoons raw sugar
½ cup water

Simmer gently until dates are very tender. Stir frequently to keep from scorching. When done, remove from heat and mash with fork. Set aside and prepare crumb mixture.

Crumb Mixture:

1 cup whole wheat pastry flour (sifted)
⅛ teaspoon salt
1 cup margarine

1 teaspoon vanilla
1 cup raw sugar (firmly packed)
2 cups rolled oats

Sift flour and salt together. Cream together, margarine, vanilla and sugar. Mix in flour and oats. Divide in half and spread one half on bottom of 8-inch square cake pan. Spread this layer with date filling. On top of date filling, spread remaining half of crumb mixture. Bake at 325° F. for 1½ hours. Cake is done when toothpick inserted in center comes out clean.

CARROT CAKE

5 carrots (sliced)
1 cup water
7 eggs (separated)
2 cups raw sugar

1 tablespoon orange rind (grated)
3 cups almonds (grated)

Cook carrots in the water until tender. Drain, saving water for soup stock. Mash carrots and let cool.

Beat egg yolks and sugar. Add the carrots, grated orange rind and almonds. Mix together. Beat egg whites until stiff, then fold into carrot

147

mixture. Pour batter into oiled 9-inch spring-form cake pan. Bake at 325° F. for about 45 minutes or until toothpick inserted in center comes out dry.

CAROB BROWNIES

¾ cup whole wheat pastry flour
1 teaspoon baking powder
½ teaspoon salt
2 eggs (beaten)
½ cup margarine (melted)
½ cup honey
½ cup carob powder mixed with 1 tablespoon melted margarine
1 cup chopped nuts or hulled sunflower seeds
1 teaspoon vanilla

Sift flour, baking powder and salt together. Beat eggs, margarine and honey together. Stir into flour. Add carob, nuts and vanilla. Mix well and spread in 9-inch square greased pan. Bake at 350° F. for 30 minutes. Do not overbake.

FRUIT CAKE

1 cup raisins
1 cup dates (pitted)
½ cup currants
½ cup figs (chopped)
3 tablespoons margarine
1 teaspoon allspice
½ teaspoon mace
½ teaspoon salt
½ cup carob powder
2 cups pastry whole wheat flour
½ cup candied pineapple
½ cup candied cherries
1 cup pignolias
1 cup pecans (chopped)

Simmer raisins, dates currants, figs and sugar in water to cover for 7 minutes. Let cool.

Sift dry ingredients together and add nuts and candied fruit. Stir in dried fruit mixture. Turn into oiled loaf pan or coffee can and bake at 300° F. for about 2 hours. Will keep for months in air-tight container.

RICE WAFFLES

2 cups rice flour
5 teaspoons baking powder
⅛ teaspoon salt

2 cups water
1 tablespoon honey
3 tablespoons sesame oil

Sift together flour, baking powder, and salt. Blend water, honey, and oil. Stir into flour mixture. Oil waffle iron well and bake.

WHOLE WHEAT EGGLESS PANCAKE BATTER

2 cups 100% stone-ground whole wheat flour (available at health food stores)
2 tablespoons soy flour
2 tablespoons soy oil
2½ cups milk

2½ teaspoons Royal baking powder (only brand not containing harmful metallic salts)
½ teaspoon cinnamon
½ teaspoon sea salt

Sift all dry ingredients together. Slowly add oil and milk, and stir gently into smooth consistency (slightly lumpy makes lighter pancakes). Bake in waffle iron, or on griddle or pan (lightly oiled) at moderate heat. (Test pan or griddle by dropping one drop of water on it. If it steams away rapidly, pan is ready). For pancakes, flip over when edges appear dry and bubbles appear in center. This batter can have blueberries added to it or similar ingredients to make your own variations.

COOKIES & CONFECTIONS

SESAME SEED COOKIES

½ cup oil or
    margarine
1 cup raw sugar
1 egg (beaten)
1 ¼ cups rolled oats
½ cup raisins

¾ cup sesame seeds
2 tablespoons milk
1 ¼ cups whole wheat
    pastry flour
½ teaspoon nutmeg

Cream oil and sugar, add egg and beat. Mix together oats, raisins, sesame seeds and milk. Stir into sugar mixture. Add sifted dry ingredients and mix well. Drop dough from teaspoon onto oiled cookie sheet. Flatten with bottom of glass or fork. Bake at 375° F. until brown.

BLACKSTRAP COOKIES

2½ cups sifted whole
   wheat pastry flour
2 teaspoons baking
   powder
1 teaspoon ginger
½ cup wheat germ

⅓ cup honey
⅔ cup blackstrap
   molasses
½ cup margarine or
   oil

Sift together the flour, baking powder, and ginger. Add wheat germ. Heat molasses until just warm enough to melt margarine. Blend in dry ingredients. Chill for an hour. Roll out on floured board and cut out shapes with floured cookie cutter. Bake at 350° F. for 10–12 minutes. Makes nice gingerbread men, too.

UNBAKED CAROB COOKIES

1 cup raisins
   (seedless)
2 cups dates (pitted)

½ cup pecans or
   pignolias
   (chopped)
Carob powder

Put raisins, dates, and nuts through food grinder. Mix in carob powder until mixture will not hold any more and dough is stiff enough to roll. Roll out and cut into bars. Place in direct sunlight for one day.

DATE CANDY

3 cups dates (pitted)
½ cup raisins

1 cup chopped pecans
   or other nuts

Grind dates and raisins in food grinder. Mix chopped nuts into fruit mixture. Knead with hands and form in a 1 inch roll. Roll in ground nuts, fine coconut, or soy grits. Wrap in wax paper and chill thoroughly. Cut into slices.

STUFFED DATES

Pitted dates may be stuffed with the following: peanut butter, blanched almonds, hulled sunflower seeds, pecans, sesame candy. Serve plain or roll in fine coconut.

SESAME FRUIT CANDY

1 lb. dried apricots
1 lb. dates
½ cup raisins or prunes
½ cup figs

½ cup plus 6 tablespoons sesame seeds
2 tablespoons creamed honey

Grind fruits in food grinder. Toast seeds as follows: Put one tablespoon sesame or soy oil in pan, add sesame seeds and shake a few minutes over medium heat with lid on (seeds pop like popcorn as they brown). Peek to see when they are golden brown. Mix fruits, seeds and honey, reserving 6 tablespoons seeds. Shape into balls and roll in remaining seeds as a covering.

SESAME CANDY

1 cup Tahini (sesame seed cream, available in health food stores, and Mediterranean delicatessens)
½ cup creamed honey
2 tablespoons coconut

¼ cup pignolias (chopped)
4 tablespoons carob powder
3 tablespoons rice polish
2 tablespoons vanilla

Mix all ingredients together. Roll in toasted sesame seeds. Coat in finely grated coconut. Chill.

TAHINI CANDY

2 tablespoons Tahini
1 cup powdered milk
½ cup crystallized or
  creamed honey

⅓ cup carob powder
¼ teaspoon vanilla

Mix all ingredients together. An easy way is to
knead the mixture with the hands. Form into a
roll, chill and slice. Slices can be coated with
finely-grated coconut or carob powder.

MOLASSES WHEAT GERM CANDY

½ cup honey
½ cup blackstrap
  molasses
1 cup raisins
1 cup peanut butter
  (crunchy)

1 cup powdered
  non-fat milk
2½ cups toasted
  wheat germ

Combine all ingredients. Knead with hands.
Press into oiled pan and cut into squares.

PASHKA
(Russian Easter Confection)

1 cup cream cheese
1 cup sour cream
½ cup currants and
  raisins
½ cup honey

½ cup soft margarine
½ cup nuts (chopped)
2 tablespoons dates
  (chopped)

Blend all ingredients together well, and press
one inch thick into pan. Chill overnight. This is
a particularly "rich" confection. The footnote
that appears beneath the Cheese Cake recipe
also applies here.

MENUS

**A sample week's menus
compiled from the
recipes of the book**

MONDAY	TUESDAY

Breakfast

Fresh orange juice	Fresh strawberries
Swiss breakfast	with yogurt and
	wheat germ
	Herb tea

Lunch

Lentil sprout salad	Sandwich:
Tomato drink	Garbanzo-Sesame
Unbaked carob cookies	spread on whole
	wheat bread
	Mint tea

Dinner

Cucumber salad	Wild rice and
Black bean soup	mushrooms
Whole wheat sesame	Beet salad
crackers	Polynesian coconut
Papaya pineapple salad	pudding

WEDNESDAY	THURSDAY

Breakfast

Whole wheat eggless waffles with apple butter or 100% pure maple syrup	Thermos bottle cooked cereal
Dish of fresh sliced pears	Fig ambrosia
	Hot carob milk drink

Lunch

Vegetable salad with natural herb dressing	Herb garden cottage cheese
Soya rice flour raisin bread with cream cheese spread	Oasis shake

Dinner

Watercress tangerine salad	Pea pods and bean sprouts
Zucchini pancakes	Bean cake and onions
Date-rice Pudding	Lemon cheese pie

FRIDAY	SATURDAY

Breakfast

Energy drink	Uncooked wheat
Whole wheat muffin	cereal with fresh
	fruit and milk
	Herb tea

Lunch

Gazpacho	Cantaloupe cup
Guacamole with	Herb tea
crackers	Sesame seed cookies

Dinner

Macaroni and cheese	Romaine salad
Raw spinach salad	Stracciatella soup
Carob brownies	Marinara sauce over
	whole wheat
	spaghetti
	Fresh fruit

SUNDAY

Breakfast

Herb tea	Freshly extracted
Enzyme Vitamin	apple juice
cereal	

Lunch

Sandwich:	Fruit juice drink
Cashew butter and	
peach butter on	
sprouted wheat	
bread	

Dinner

Tossed green salad	Ratatouille
with kelp dressing	Berry yogurt

RECIPE INDEX

157

Readers who wish to correspond with Mr. Hittleman regarding the application of Yoga Nutrition to their personal needs may write directly to:

Richard Hittleman—
Carmel Valley, Calif. 93924